TEACHING
COMPUTING
UNPLUGGED
IN PRIMARY SCHOOLS

SAGE was founded in 1965 by Sara Miller McCune to support the dissemination of usable knowledge by publishing innovative and high-quality research and teaching content. Today, we publish over 900 journals, including those of more than 400 learned societies, more than 800 new books per year, and a growing range of library products including archives, data, case studies, reports, and video. SAGE remains majority-owned by our founder, and after Sara's lifetime will become owned by a charitable trust that secures our continued independence.

Los Angeles | London | New Delhi | Singapore | Washington DC | Melbourne

HELEN CALDWELL + NEIL SMITH

TEACHING COMPUTING UNPLUGGED
IN PRIMARY SCHOOLS

exploring primary computing
through practical activities
away from the computer

Learning Matters
An imprint of SAGE Publications Ltd
1 Oliver's Yard
55 City Road
London EC1Y 1SP

SAGE Publications Inc.
2455 Teller Road
Thousand Oaks, California 91320

SAGE Publications India Pvt Ltd
B 1/I 1 Mohan Cooperative Industrial Area
Mathura Road
New Delhi 110 044

SAGE Asia-Pacific Pte Ltd
3 Church Street
#10–04 Samsung Hub
Singapore 049483

Editor: Amy Thornton
Development editor: Geoff Barker
Production editor: Chris Marke
Marketing manager: Lorna Patkai
Cover design: Wendy Scott
Typeset by: C&M Digitals (P) Ltd, Chennai, India
Printed and bound by CPI Group (UK) Ltd,
Croydon, CR0 4YY

First published in 2017 by Learning Matters Ltd.

© 2017 Helen Caldwell and Neil Smith

Library of Congress Control Number: 2016944011

British Library Cataloguing in Publication Data

A catalogue record for this book is available from the
British Library

ISBN: 978-1-4739-6169-2 (hbk)
ISBN: 978-1-4739-6170-8 (pbk)

At SAGE we take sustainability seriously. Most of our products are printed in the UK using FSC papers and boards.
When we print overseas we ensure sustainable papers are used as measured by the PREPS grading system.
We undertake an annual audit to monitor our sustainability.

CONTENTS

ABOUT THE AUTHORS AND CONTRIBUTORS

Authors

Helen Caldwell is a Senior Lecturer in the Teacher Education Division at the University of Northampton, where she is curriculum lead for Primary Computing and programme lead for the Postgraduate Certificate in Primary Computing. Her teaching covers the use of technology across primary subjects, implementing the computing curriculum and assistive technologies for SEND. She offers CPD for teachers and Initial Teacher Training across these areas. Her PhD research focuses on the transfer of innovative pedagogies in technology education within professional learning communities.

Neil Smith is a Senior Lecturer in the Computing and Communications department of The Open University and leads the department's school outreach activity. His research is mainly on computer science education and artificial intelligence; he teaches introductory undergraduate computing and data analysis. He has worked with Code Club, Computing At School, and the BCS on how to deliver computer science and computational thinking in schools. He has trained CAS Master Teachers and is an assessor for the BCS Certificate of Computer Science Teaching.

Contributors

Sway Grantham is a primary school teacher and a Specialist Leader in Education (SLE) for the Milton Keynes area. She has been ICT/Computing Leader since her NQT year and during this time has written a new curriculum and conducted research into the impact of 1:1 iPads in the primary classroom. Sway has been using technology all her life and has spent the last five years focusing this on education. She was invited as a 'lead learner' to attend the first ever Raspberry Picademy, becoming a Raspberry Pi Certified Teacher, and loves the opportunities these cheap computers offer. Recently having qualified as a Google Certified Teacher, Sway believes in offering children a range of ICT and Computing opportunities. Over the years, Sway has built up a successful blog (**www.swaygrantham.co.uk**), which is full of learning ideas and pedagogy for Computing, ICT and many other curriculum areas.

Scott Turner is currently an Associate Professor of Computing and Immersive Technologies and Deputy Subject Leader for Computing at the University of Northampton. He has published over thirty papers on pedagogy in computing in

Higher Education, including the teaching of programming and problem-solving. He is also a STEM Ambassador, Pi Certified Educator and Code Club volunteer at two Code Clubs. Since 2009, Dr Turner has also being running a project called Junkbots, which includes turning 'junk' into moving bots.

Katharine Childs is currently working as a Code Club Regional Manager for the Raspberry Pi Foundation. Her previous roles include 15 years working in IT support and network management in the private and educational sectors, before then going on to share her knowledge as a teacher of computing in primary schools. She has an undergraduate degree in IT & Computing and is now undertaking an MSc in Computing in Education. Katharine is an advocate for offering children access to high-quality computer science opportunities and presented a rigorous case for this in her TEDx talk 'Coding the Hairy Toe' in April 2015.

Kim Calvert is a primary school teacher currently working in a SEN school. She previously worked in a primary school for five years before moving into special needs teaching. Computing coordinator at Billing Brook School, Northampton, she has been actively developing and improving the computing curriculum to ensure it is both creative and effective. She is passionate about using technology to support creativity within the classroom (not just within the computing subject) and believes in the value of Unplugged Computing to embed computational thinking within pupils' learning. She has worked with Barefoot to develop a number of unplugged SEN teaching resources which are available on their website and has delivered numerous training sessions to promote the use of Unplugged Computing. She is a Computing SLE for Northants as well as being a CAS Master Teacher and Raspberry Pi Certified Educator. **kimcalvert@billingbrook.northants.sch.uk**

Mark Dorling is the former National CPD Coordinator for Computing At School (CAS) funded by the Department for Education (DfE), but he is probably best known for his work in the Digital Schoolhouse project at Langley Grammar School that gained him national and international recognition. Mark is a primary-trained teacher with many years of both primary and secondary teaching, teacher training and industry experience. He played a leading role in developing the 2014 Computing Programmes of Study, CAS computational thinking guidance for teachers and the highly popular CAS Computing Progression Pathways framework. More recently, he was involved in the DfE consultation on 'Assessment without levels' and is currently part of the team setting up the Ian Livingstone Academies.

Paul Curzon is a Professor of Computer Science at Queen Mary University of London. His research interests are computer science education, human computer interaction and formal methods. He was awarded a Higher Education Academy National Teaching Fellowship in 2010 and won the EPSRC Non-professional Computer Science Writer of the Year in 2007. He co-founded Teaching London Computing (**www. teachinglondoncomputing.org**), providing CPD support for teachers.

Peter W. McOwan is also a Professor of Computer Science at Queen Mary University of London. His research interests are in computer vision, artificial intelligence and robotics. He was awarded a Higher Education Academy National Teaching Fellowship in 2008 and the IET Mountbatten medal in 2011 for his work in promoting computer science to diverse audiences. Paul and Peter co-created the internationally known Computer Science for fun project (**www.cs4fn.org**) and were original members of the UK Computing at School network, of which Paul is now a board member.

Yasemin Allsop worked as an ICT Coordinator in primary schools in London for almost ten years. In 2014, she started to work as a senior lecturer in Computing at Manchester Metropolitan University, also running CPD sessions in Computing at the MMU STEM centre. She is currently employed as a Senior Lecturer in Computing Education at Roehampton University. Her research focus is children's thinking, learning and metacognition when designing digital games. She is the founder and co-editor of an online magazine called *ICT in Practice* (**www.ictinpractice.com**) where educators from around the world share their experiences of using technology in education. She is the EU Code Week ambassador for the UK, and also co-edits *International Journal of Computer Science Education in Schools*. Her last book, with Ben Sedman, is called *Primary Computing in Action*. **www.yaseminallsop.me.uk**

Jane Waite is an experienced primary teacher with over ten years' classroom experience. She spent twenty years working in the IT sector before moving into teaching. Jane worked on the Barefoot Computing project creating cross-curricula activities and concept explanations that demystify computational thinking. She writes for cs4fn, Cambridge International and Primary Computing, provides CPD and presents at conferences around the country. Jane also works for King's College London and Queen Mary University London as the Computing At School regional project manager for London and undertakes research in computer science education.

Jon Chippindall is a part-time primary school teacher at Crumpsall Lane Primary School, Manchester, where he specialises in teaching computing and science. Jon was an author of the DfE-funded Barefoot Computing resources, which have helped thousands of teachers across the country deliver computer science in their schools. Jon is a CAS Master Teacher and runs the computing blog **www.primarycomputing. co.uk**. He is also visiting academic at The University of Manchester, where he leads on innovative computing and engineering education in primary schools and supports the computing teacher training programme.

ACKNOWLEDGEMENTS

INTRODUCTION: COMPUTING UNPLUGGED

Teaching 'Computing' is now a fact of life for all schools in England, and soon to be the same across the UK and elsewhere. It is a subject with lofty goals: *a high-quality computing education equips pupils to use computational thinking and creativity to understand and change the world* (Programmes of Study, 2013, **www.gov.uk/government/publications/national-curriculum-in-england-computing-programmes-of-study**).

This book is about a way of teaching computing without using computers. Each of the chapters shows how central concepts in computing and computational thinking can be explored and developed away from technology. Each chapter is based around a different theme and shows how thinking like a computer scientist can be illustrated by everyday activities, and how it can help us solve problems in many different situations. This approach should give children and teachers a deeper understanding of computing, and how and why it can be applied to more than just programming. The lesson ideas model how computational thinking can be embedded across the curriculum.

Computing

Computing is a subject with three strands: digital literacy, information technology and computer science (Shut Down or Restart, Royal Society, 2012, **https://royalsociety.org/topics-policy/projects/computing-in-schools/report/**). Digital literacy is about creating, evaluating and using digital artefacts. Information technology is about how computers work, work together and can be made to work. Computer science is about the essence of what computing *is*: what can be computed, and how to think about problems and solutions with a view to applying them to computers. In this sense, it's not really *about* computers: rather it's about how to think. Therefore, one key aim of teaching computing is about getting children to think about the world in a different way.

Viewed this way, we can see that 'computing' isn't about computers in the same way that 'science' isn't about test tubes and 'art' isn't about paintbrushes. Computers, test tubes and paintbrushes are all vitally important tools we use in these different disciplines, and we have to understand them and how to use them effectively. But there's much more to art and science than just the tools, and there's much more to computing than just computers and programming.

This book is an approach to the discipline of computing that does away with computers. By removing the distraction of computers, we can instead concentrate on the essence of computing and learn how to apply computational thinking techniques to a range of different problems.

Computational thinking

When the current Computing curriculum was introduced, everyone was very exercised by 'programming' and 'coding'. This, people thought, was the key skill required by the new curriculum. However, just understanding the particular syntax rules of a particular programming language is neither interesting nor particularly useful on its own.

Programming is much like bricklaying: you need to know a little bit about it to be able to build something, and master artisans can have long and detailed conversations about pointing and the relative advantages of variations on herringbone layouts, but fundamentally a wall is a wall. Bricklaying isn't that interesting: *architecture* is interesting. Just as architecture is about understanding people's requirements and seeing how a particularly shaped pile of bricks could address them, *computational thinking* is about understanding a problem and seeing how a particularly shaped pile of program statements could address it.

Computational thinking has many definitions. Jeanette Wing (2006, Computational thinking *Communications of the ACM* 49 (3): 33. doi:10.1145/1118178.1118215)

Figure i The computational thinker

Table i Six concepts and five approaches

Concepts: key ideas and methods of thought	Approaches: ways of approaching, tackling, and solving problems
Logic: thinking in terms of rules, applying them to situations, and getting a result.	*Tinkering*: trying things, seeing what works. Exploring.
Algorithms: defined sequences of steps that achieve some result.	*Creating*: making something new and innovative, but purposefully.
Decomposition: breaking a problem down into smaller steps, and solving each in turn.	*Debugging*: spotting mistakes and fixing them.
Finding and using *patterns*: seeing how a previous solution or approach can be applied here.	*Persevering*: not giving up when the first attempt fails.
Abstraction: finding what's important, discarding the unimportant, to keep attention on what really matters.	*Collaborating*: working together, sharing ideas, and building something together.
Evaluation: not only deciding if something works, but deciding what 'works' means in this situation.	

resurrected and redefined the term in 2006 as 'Ways to Think Like a Computer Scientist'. Her idea was elastic and stretched to many definitions. In this book, we use the definition of computational thinking defined by Barefoot (2014) (**http://barefootcas.org.uk/barefoot-primary-computing-resources/concepts/computational-thinking/**) and *Computational thinking – A guide for teachers* (Csizmadia *et al.* 2015, **http://community.computingatschool.org.uk/resources/2324**)

This is a constellation of six concepts and five approaches. As children develop and master these concepts and approaches, they are better able to grasp a range of problems and develop robust, efficient solutions to them. Very often, these solutions won't involve computers, in much the same way that science is more about a way of thinking and understanding (the scientific method) than any particular fact.

A quick look at these concepts and approaches shows that they are generally useful and applicable across a range of subjects and activities. Computing is a place where these ideas come to the fore, but it's not the only place where they're useful.

This book is about computational thinking. It's about developing these computational thinking skills in students and helping them apply the skills in different situations across the curriculum.

Becoming unplugged

When computational thinking is the central activity in computing, the computers themselves become just a tool for carrying out the processes we've designed elsewhere. From this point of view, the computer can become a distraction. Getting the technology to work can be a fiddly and time-consuming process: we have all at some point spent far too long tweaking the layout of a document to make it look just right rather than doing something productive.

It is much more difficult to learn a new skill such as computational thinking while dealing with unfamiliar and recalcitrant technology. We have to expend mental effort to practise the new skill while simultaneously trying to operate a device. This combination can easily overwhelm the best of us.

What can be much more useful for learners is to step away from the technology and practise the computational thinking skills in a different setting. If the physical trappings of the new setting are simple and well-known, such as pencil and paper, beanbags and hoops, we don't need to devote any energy to making them work and can instead focus on the new skills and knowledge we are developing: the computational thinking skills and any subject-specific knowledge and vocabulary. Once we've acquired the new abilities, we can apply them to a computing technology, confident that we know what we are trying to achieve and how to go about it; the only difficulty is inherent in the technology, not in us.

Unplugged activities also engage learners in different modalities. Very often, we interact with computing devices by sitting still, looking at a screen, and manipulating keyboard, mouse and touchscreen. This emphasises visual, logical and mathematical modes of reasoning but leaves out many other modes. Children, especially young children, find it difficult to sit still for long periods, even more so when they're restricted to just a few modes of interaction. The activities in this book explore a much wider range of activity, including musical, kinaesthetic, artistic, intrapersonal and interpersonal (see Gardner, 2011). This variety should assist you with engaging with all the students in your class and maintaining that engagement.

Pedagogy

The playful nature of many of these unplugged activities emphasises the constructivist pedagogy that underlies this approach. Away from the computer, and the performance anxiety and stress it could cause, learners are free to experiment and explore the activity and the thinking that underlies it. This will help them construct their own understanding of the topic, assisted by suitable scaffolding from the teacher. The physical nature of many of the unplugged tasks results in learners making some artefact that either embodies or represents their learning, such as a written-out, debugged algorithm or even a bowl of fruit salad, thus supporting both Papert's constructionism and Piaget's constructivism (see Ackerman, 2001).

The collaborative nature of many of the activities encourages social constructivism, with learners developing, testing and refining their ideas together in a social setting (Vygotsky, 1980).

By definition, computing unplugged develops skills in one context (unplugged) that must be applied to another (plugged, using the technology). While this requires more of the learners than simply learning a new skill to be applied in the same context, it should develop more metacognitive awareness in learners as they apply existing learning to a new context and talk about the transfer of skills.

Computing, despite its abstract and mathematical basis, is a strongly practical activity. Going back to an earlier analogy, one does not become a competent bricklayer from just reading about it: competence only comes from direct activity. All the approaches of computational thinking are active ones, requiring engagement and interaction by the learner. Most of the activities in this book have a strong experiential flavour, with the learners moving through Kolb's (2014) experiential learning cycle at least once in the activity.

Cross-curricular links

As we said earlier, computational thinking is a general approach to thinking about and tackling problems. While it is most apparent and distinctive when it comes to computing, the same concepts and approaches are present in many disciplines and subjects. We are seeing this in the wider world, with computers and smart devices moving into many areas from fitness tracking and photography to romance and autonomous transport.

Computing can apply to other domains in two different, but complementary, ways. The digital literacy strand of computing is about the ability to use technology tools to assist the normal practice of a discipline, such as providing new tools for drawing and manipulating images. This is one way that people think computing can be applied to the world.

But computational thinking provides a different approach. It can be used as a lens through which to view a subject, such as understanding a piece of art by crafting an algorithm that can create it, or finding a new recipe for fruit salad by finding the common and distinct elements of a range of existing ones.

Here are a few cross-curricular examples:

- *Numeracy*: many standard calculations (addition, division) can be expressed as algorithms. Patterns can be found in relating things like properties of shapes. Co-ordinates can be illustrated by making 'robots' move (see Chapter 1).

- *Literacy*: algorithms are often written as sets of instructions, which must be clear and precise. Phonics have rules for how sounds are written and how letters make sounds.

- *Art and Design*: art often abstracts details away from life to create a representation. Making complex pieces can be decomposed into a sequence of steps.

- *Science*: performing experiments requires following algorithms. Making predictions and drawing deductions from them is making patterns and involves logical thinking.

- *Geography*: algorithms appear as ways to find, communicate and follow directions. Grid references are co-ordinates and, again, can be used to move people or objects around a map.

- *History*: the small details of a period of history can be abstracted away to see the broader sweep, with events grouped into periods.

- *PE*: rules of sports are full of algorithms and decision-making processes, which can be drawn out as algorithms. Dances are sequences of movements and can be analysed similarly to songs (see Chapter 3).

- *PSHE*: We all follow algorithms for staying healthy, follow routines when entering or leaving school, and so on. When things go wrong, the processes can be debugged to make them better or find where problems arose.

About this book

Each chapter in this book explores how computational thinking relates to a different activity. The topics were chosen to show the range of applications of computational thinking, and to draw out important aspects of it. Above all, the topics are meant to be fun and engaging.

The activities throughout the chapters in this book show a large number of ways that computational thinking can be used across the curriculum, such as through drama, the outdoors, art, music, puzzles, games and practical hands-on activities. We suggest ways of tackling computer science concepts in a collaborative way by taking on the roles of robots, musicians, artists, explorers, code breakers, magicians, gamers, cooks and scientists. This demonstrates that computational thinking techniques can be applied across curriculum subjects so that they are embedded as a creative problem-solving tool.

Each chapter follows a similar format. It starts by outlining the key computational thinking aspects that are developed and explored in that chapter, including key terms and concepts used. There are three classroom activities presented as outline lesson plans that give concrete examples of how the concepts can be explored in a classroom setting. Sections discussing the computational thinking aspects in more detail and inviting you to reflect on other ways they can be incorporated into your teaching follow these. There is some discussion of pedagogical strategies for implementing the activities across a range of age groups and abilities, along with suggestions for extension activities and for follow-on 'plugged' activities using a range of free online resources. Examples are given of how the concepts are relevant in real-world situations such as medical devices or weather forecasting. This reinforces the idea that a computing lesson or set of lessons might introduce concepts through an unplugged activity, apply them via some 'plugged' digital making and also give consideration to their use in real-world contexts.

Resources

Computing in the national curriculum: a guide for primary teachers. **www.computingatschool.org.uk/data/uploads/CASPrimaryComputing.pdf**

Computing in the national curriculum: a guide for secondary teachers. **www.computingatschool.org.uk/data/uploads/cas_secondary.pdf**

Computer Science in a Box: Unplug your curriculum. A set of seven unplugged lesson ideas from the National Center for Women and Information Technology (**ncwit.org**) **www.ncwit.org/sites/default/files/resources/computerscience-in-a-box.pdf**

References

Ackermann, E (2001) Piaget's constructivism, Papert's constructionism: What's the difference. *Future of learning group publication*, 5(3), 438.

Gardner, H (2011). Frames of mind: The theory of multiple intelligences. Basic Books.

Kolb, DA (2014) *Experiential Learning: Experience as the source of learning and development.* FT Press.

Vygotsky, LS (1980). *Mind in Society: The development of higher psychological processes.* Harvard University Press.

Chapter 1

ROBOTS

The good news about computers is that they do what you tell them to do. The bad news is that they do what you tell them to do.

Ted Nelson

Introduction

This chapter is all about learning through action. We suggest that children make and execute programs with their bodies and their voices: jumping, skipping, climbing, crawling and yelling instructions. Instead of programming being trapped behind a glass computer screen, they will learn some fundamental computing concepts by working with real human robots. Our activities encourage children to work in teams to develop sequences of commands and then test them out on each other by role-playing robot movements. The idea is that cementing the computing concepts through fun hands-on kinaesthetic experiences will help to transfer them to written code scenarios.

Programming is about giving clear instructions and having someone or something carry them out. Robots are good things to program because it is easy to watch the program being executed in real life and then to evaluate the effectiveness of the algorithm. People can make good robots because they can interpret (and misinterpret) natural language instructions. Their misinterpretations can add a good deal of humour to a lesson and make the process of debugging entertaining and memorable. Human robots are also readily available in a classroom for no additional cost.

The physical world is a safe and accessible place to play with lines of code, make mistakes and rearrange sequences of instructions. This makes it easier to develop computational thinking skills without technology getting in the way. By programming each other, children are supporting through collaboration, reinforcing the fact that coding can be an engaging problem-solving activity and that it can even take place in the playground.

As your pupils develop their programs, they will recognise the need for instructions to be clear and precise, at the appropriate level of detail and sufficiently flexible to deal with different but related situations. You will be helping them to understand that computing is about logical and creative problem solving. You will also be developing their ability to talk about the ways in which they are applying computational thinking skills to devise workable solutions.

Importantly, when children see how their routines work in the physical world, it often happens that they spontaneously reinvent more complex algorithmic structures such as repetition and selection. They may naturally introduce repeat loops (iterative statements) and decision making using if-then sentences (conditional statements) into the sequences of instructions for their human robots. Finding out about these logical processes for themselves rather than just being told about them is a powerful learning opportunity. If they make these discoveries while composing their own algorithms, they understand the concepts more deeply and are likely to be able to transfer them to other problem-solving situations.

Learning Outcomes

At the end of this chapter you should be able to:

- specify the operations that can be used to perform a task and assemble them into an algorithm
- design and lead a computing unplugged activity for your class that helps children to understand that programmers need to write precise sequences of instructions;
- identify and build upon children's natural use of computing concepts such as loops and decision making in the context of programming human robots.

Links to Teachers' Standards

The following Teachers' Standards are particularly relevant to this chapter:

TS2d Demonstrate knowledge and understanding of how pupils learn.
TS2e Encourage pupils to take a responsible and conscientious attitude to their own work.
TS3a Have a secure knowledge of the relevant subject(s) and curriculum areas, foster and maintain pupils' interest in the subject.
TS4a Promote a love of learning and children's intellectual curiosity.
TS4e Contribute to the design and provision of an engaging curriculum.

(DfE, 2011)

Links to National Curriculum Programmes of Study

Key Stage 1

- Understand what algorithms are, how they are implemented as programs on digital devices, and that programs execute by following precise and unambiguous instructions.
- Create and debug simple programs.
- Use logical reasoning to predict the behaviour of simple programs.

Key Stage 2

- Design, write and debug programs that accomplish specific goals, including controlling or simulating physical systems; solve problems by decomposing them into smaller parts.
- Use sequence, selection, and repetition in programs; work with variables and various forms of input and output.
- Use logical reasoning to explain how some simple algorithms work and to detect and correct errors in algorithms and programs.

(DfE, 2013)

Need to know

Here we will think about the subject knowledge that is relevant to this chapter.

First, it is important for children to understand that computers solve problems by following sets of instructions and that they follow the instructions literally. The set of instructions that solves the problem or completes the task is the algorithm. An algorithm consists of a step-by-step sequence of operations. A program is a particular way of writing an algorithm so that both a human and a computer can understand it. Programs can be written in different languages. For example, '*Go to your room and eat a banana*' and '*Geh in dein Zimmer und essen eine Banane*' use different languages to express the same algorithm.

There are many different computer languages but they are all based on the need to give precise and unambiguous instructions. A programming language is a way of coding actions using a limited vocabulary and a symbolic language.

Errors in computer programs are known as bugs, and the story goes that they are named after a moth that was removed from a calculating machine in 1947 (see Figure 1.1). Errors in computer programs can have devastating consequences and so software needs to be tested methodically. The process of evaluating and improving algorithms is known as debugging.

Algorithms sometimes contain choices. Conditional statements (also known as IF statements) direct computers to choose which branch of an algorithm to run. They help computers to make decisions based on the idea that the condition is true or false. In computing, these true or false choices are known as Boolean values. They are similar to many everyday situations, for example 'IF it is raining THEN put on your coat'. It is easy to find real-life examples of conditional statements during the school day, such as taking the register or lining up for playtime.

We can also repeat sections of algorithms. Iteration statements are also known as REPEAT statements, WHILE statements, or FOR statements. They tell the computer to loop over the same set of instructions. Sometimes we use loops just to make the program simpler ('REPEAT 5; step forward' versus 'step forward; step forward; step forward; step forward; step forward'). Sometimes we use loops to make part of an algorithm run a different number of times depending on the situation. Again, we can

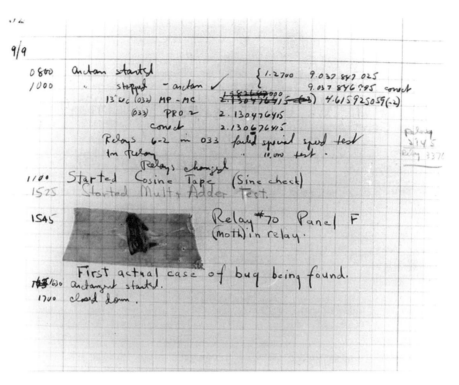

Figure 1.1 The moth and the calculating machine

think of real-life examples to illustrate the logic; 'WHILE there are books to mark; DO take the top book; mark it'.

Algorithms themselves are often very simple. What can make them challenging to write is insufficient understanding of the problem we are trying to solve. One very powerful technique to craft algorithms is to sneak up on them, like this:

write a program to solve just the first bit of the problem

run the program

WHILE the program isn't fully working

WHILE there are bugs

fix the bug

run the program

add some more program to solve the next little bit

run the program

Yes, this is an algorithm for writing algorithms. This cycle of 'run – test – fix – add' also shows the creative and exploratory nature of much computing. It makes the problem easier to solve by decomposing it into smaller chunks and testing these one at a time.

This software-developing process checks small sections of the program at a time. You write a few steps, run, fix, run again and then add a bit more until you have a working sequence. In the context of computing, evaluation means making judgements about programs in order to improve them.

The Introduction has more discussion about computational thinking and how algorithms and programming fit into the National Curriculum.

Two good sources of further information about computational thinking are the CAS computational thinking guide for teachers **http://community.computingatschool. org.uk/resources/2324** and the Barefoot Computing resources **http://barefootcas. org.uk/resources**. Both guides are free but you will need to create a login for the websites.

We suggest three lesson ideas for developing the theme of human robots in primary classrooms:

- *Robot hamster playground*: learning about sequencing algorithms based on symbolic representation.

- *Shoot the robot*: using defined commands to construct algorithms to achieve a goal.

- *Robot foodies*: learning to persevere and debug algorithms to solve a problem.

Unplugged Activity 1: Robot hamster playground

Overview

In this activity children design a playground for a robot hamster and take turns at programming each other to explore it. They use an invented notation for the commands that helps them to make a connection between symbols and actions.

At the beginning of the lesson children explore what they already know about how computers work by considering the question, 'Can computers think?' It is a natural reaction to assume that computers are clever, so it is worth spending some time building understanding that they operate by following a set of instructions and that this is called an algorithm. Children will also learn that the same algorithm can be written down in different ways, each of which is a different program. They evaluate the effectiveness of a sequence of instructions and gain understanding that computers need programming with very specific instructions as they are unable to think for themselves. Finally, they make improvements to their algorithms through the process of debugging. The lesson will take around 60 minutes.

Cross-curricular links

Mathematics
Key Stage 1:

- Use mathematical vocabulary to describe position, direction and movement.

- Distinguish between rotation as a turn and in terms of right angles.

Key Stage 2:

- Recognise angles as a description of a turn.

Design and Technology
Key Stages 1 and 2:

- Generate, develop, model and communicate their ideas.

Key Stage 2:

- Generate, develop, model and communicate their ideas.

- Apply their understanding of computing.

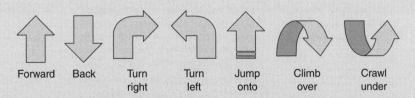

| Forward | Back | Turn right | Turn left | Jump onto | Climb over | Crawl under |

Figure 1.2 A possible notation for moving through an obstacle course

Age range

This activity is aimed at Years 2–4, but it could be adapted to work across the primary age range.

Lesson plan

Learning objectives

To create algorithms based on symbolic representation in order to solve a problem.

To use debugging and evaluation skills to improve an algorithm.

'I can' statements:

- I can design a programming challenge.
- I can decompose a sequence of moves into a set of parts.
- I can create an algorithm using symbols.
- I can debug my code to make it work better.
- I can evaluate the changes I made to my code.

Key words and questions

algorithm, debugging, code, program, malfunction, repeat, execute program, stored procedure, repetition, loop, conditional statement

- Can computers think?

- How can we represent movements as symbols?

- How can we tell whether our algorithm works?

- How can we develop a method of testing and fixing our algorithm?

- Can we describe any ways in which we have improved our algorithms?

- What have we learned about the ways in which computers solve problems?

Activities

Time	Teacher activity	Student activity	Resources
10 mins	Begin by introducing the question, 'Can computers think?' Present some images from a Google search of 'hamster playground'.	Think-pair-share what we already know about computers. Discuss what makes a good hamster playground. Pic Collage out some ideas on flipchart paper in small groups. Annotate with words to describe the hamster movements: e.g. jump, climb, tunnel, burrow, drop, rotate, turn, squat, swing, nibble, scurry. Alternatively, annotate one of the Google images using Pic Collage on an iPad.	Paper and pens or tablets and an image. An annotation app such as Pic Collage.

Time	Teacher activity	Student activity	Resources
10 mins	Review pupils' ideas. Introduce the idea of creating a hamster playground using simple resources and programming each other to role-play the hamster's movements.	Invent a notation for the commands using symbols such as up and down arrows, curved arrows, circles and other regular shapes. Pupils produce a key for their symbols.	A set of laminated command cards to provide extra support.
25 mins	Carry out the role-play.	Groups of pupils set up obstacle stations that combine into a course. In partners, students write the commands for their part of the obstacle course. Run the program with pairs taking turns to role-play the hamsters.	Chairs, desks, blankets, cones, PE apparatus, etc.
10 mins	Introduce the idea of debugging the code.	Debug the code, swap roles and re-run the program.	
5 mins	Evaluate which improvements were successful. Discuss how the activity relates to computer programming.	Think-pair-share: what do we now know about computers?	

Variations, differentiation and extensions

Differentiation

Some students might struggle to invent an appropriate range of symbols or might create them at an inappropriate level of detail. For example, 'Do the obstacle course' or 'Move your left foot forward', instead of 'Take a step'. You might provide extra support through laminated notation cards and suggested vocabulary. You could also consider supporting by organising your pairs to include different abilities.

Able students could consider how to make their code shorter and more efficient by using loops for repeated actions, e.g. 'move forward five steps' or 'move forward until the next obstacle'. Or they could use conditional (if-then) statements for moving beyond space boundaries, e.g. 'If on edge bounce'.

If there are repeated obstacles at different stages of the course, you could prompt more able students to bundle up the commands for a particular obstacle into a procedure that can be called when that obstacle is reached. For instance, if the course had a 'step over then crawl under' obstacle at the start and the end, the instructions for navigating that obstacle could be placed in a procedure and called at the appropriate places in the overall algorithm. Computer applications are programmed to 'call' stored procedures in order to execute them.

Extensions

1. The LightBot app (**https://lightbot.com**) uses a simple set of instructions to move a robot around an obstacle course.

2. Rather than moving through an obstacle course, the instructions could be to make a tower out of coloured blocks as in the 'human crane' activity from Code-it.co.uk (**http://code-it.co.uk/ks1/crane/humancrane**). This unplugged activity goes well with the app CargoBot.

Plugged activities

Children could follow on from the unplugged activity by creating an obstacle course for BeeBots with tunnels and enemies to avoid.

Then they could move into a plugged environment and design a hamster playground or maze within Scratch using the arrow keys to control their sprite. A search on Scratch using the term 'hamster playground' will give you some examples to remix. Analysis of how others have written Scratch code to solve similar problems will help children to develop the computational thinking skills of generalisation and pattern recognition.

There are some useful Scratch help cards on how to control a sprite using the arrow keys or mouse **https://scratch.mit.edu/help/cards**. A variation of the activity would be for children to create a sprite out of a photograph of a pet and design a playground for it in Scratch. You will need to show them how to use the Erase tool with Zoom in Scratch to remove unwanted parts of their photo in order to make the pet sprite.

An alternative project theme might be to make your own crazy golf course in real life and then replicate it in Scratch.

Success criteria and assessment

- All children have written a sequence of instructions using invented notation.

- Most children have debugged their sequence of instructions.

- Some children will be able to evaluate what makes a good sequence of instructions.

You can check whether pupils have met the learning outcomes by looking at the instructions they produce rather than how well they navigate the obstacles. Another way of testing the quality of the instructions is to ask pupils to swap the algorithms between groups and see how well they navigate the course. Children will annotate their written code to show how they debugged it. They should be able to explain that computers follow instructions literally whereas people use common sense.

Unplugged Activity 2: Shoot the robot

Overview

This activity takes the form of a robot team game with teams shouting 'forward', 'turn' and 'fire' commands to a blindfolded human robot in order to get them to throw a ball to hit their opponent. It is adapted from the Computing At School (CAS) activity 'Stompy Zombie Robots'. Children learn to translate physical activities into instructions and then code them using a limited set of commands.

Cross-curricular links

Mathematics
Key Stage 1:

● Use mathematical vocabulary to describe position, direction and movement.

● Distinguish between rotation as a turn and in terms of right angles.

Key Stage 2:

● Recognise angles as a description of a turn.

Age range

This activity could be adapted for use across the primary age range.

Lesson plan

Learning outcomes

To be able to create an algorithm from a defined set of commands.

To refine the use of commands to create a precise sequence of instructions that achieve a goal.

'I can' statements:

● I can create a simple program.
● I can give instructions from a small set.
● I can use logical reasoning to achieve a goal.
● I can improve upon my ideas through trial and error.

Need to know

Something children might struggle with when pretending to be a robot is confusing interpreting the instructions in the way that they 'should' be taken with following the precise instructions given. They may need to practise listening carefully and following the instructions exactly as given.

Key words and questions

algorithm, command, sequence, problem decomposition, procedure, automation, decision-making, flowchart, logic

- How do we talk to robots and how can they understand what we want them to do?

- Can robots play games?

- Can we work out a sequence of commands that represents a successful game strategy?

Activities

Time	Teacher activity	Student activity	Resources
5 mins	Share some images of robots and ask whether anyone has interacted with a robot. How do we 'talk' to robots? How do they understand us?	Think-pair-share on what we already know about interacting with robots.	Slideshow or laminated images.
15 mins	Explain the game. Small groups of children control one blindfolded human robot with the aim of being the first to get a ball to hit a target or to hit the robot of the opposing team. The robot can only understand a limited number of commands, e.g. Forward, Turn, Fire.	Pupils nominate a robot. The rest of the group gives instructions. When the robot is within shooting distance they use the command fire aiming to be the first to get their ball to hit the target or land in the box. Once a robot is hit it can't reload. The first group to hit their target with the ball wins round one. In round two the teams aim to get their robot to fire at the robot of the opposing team.	Scrunched-up paper balls or light plastic balls. Blindfold. A box or target.
10 mins	Allow the teams to invent their own secret command and replay the game.	The secret command might allow their robot to rise up and down, to move backwards, to zoom to another position or to use a protective shield.	
20 mins	Discuss what were the most successful strategies.	Pupils devise flowcharts to demonstrate the sequence of commands that represents their most successful game strategy.	Example flowchart.

Variations, differentiation and extensions

Differentiation

The game can be played with or without a blindfold. You can also vary the size of balls and boxes to vary the level of difficulty.

The game can be made more complex by increasing the range of possible commands.

As in Activity 1, you may find that pupils naturally introduce selection and repetition into their sequences of commands, providing you with a context for teaching these concepts.

Extensions

1. Pupils could design an obstacle course and write instructions for completing it with one blindfolded pupil acting as a robot and their partner as the programmer navigating the robot.

2. The paper BeeBot commands available from Barefoot Computing (see BeeBots 1, 2, 3 Activity) could be used for pupils to program each other. This could be an unplugged prelude to working with real BeeBots.

3. You could move from the game into using the robot to hunt for a hidden treasure in the room.

4. A variation that continues the game theme is to create and use a set of commands to organise a human snakes and ladders game in the playground.

Plugged activities

1. An idea that leads into a plugged activity is to make a cardboard robot arm out of junk boxes and invent a sequence of commands to program it to pick up an object. Following on from this, children could program a simulated robot arm using Scratch. All the instructions, materials and sample Scratch project for this Cardboard2Code activity are available free from CBiS Education: **www.cbis. education/cardboard2code_module1.aspx**

2. The Scratch website has a set of starter project games with suggestions for remix ideas: **https://scratch.mit.edu/starter_projects**. You could follow the unplugged robot game activity with a carousel of these to explore. The Scratch projects are very well supported by example remixes so that your pupils will be able to work independently.

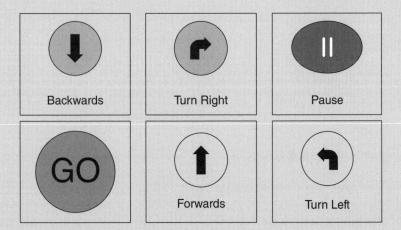

Figure 1.3 Paper commands for programming a human robot

Success criteria and assessment

- All children have used a string of commands to control a human robot.

- Most children have invented additional commands and incorporated them into the game.

- Some children have represented their game strategy as a flowchart.

You will be able to use targeted questioning at the beginning and end of the lesson to assess children's prior knowledge, misconceptions and developing understanding about creating algorithms to control robotic movements. Pupils' flowcharts will demonstrate their ability to use logical reasoning.

Unplugged Activity 3: Robot foodies

Overview

In this activity, pupils program their robot teacher to make a food item and then go on to invent an algorithm for a snack of their choice. This could be toast, a poached egg, a salad, a cup of tea, snack noodles, an ice-cream float, a bowl of cereal, a fruit salad or fruit kebab, a milk shake, a smoothie or a sandwich, for example. They command the robot to make the snack by calling out instructions which the robot follows to the letter, intentionally misinterpreting the instructions at times in order to reinforce the idea that computers follow commands literally. This can lead to an entertaining lesson.

The objective of this activity is for children to realise that robots, and hence computers, are very simple machines and need very clear instructions in order to perform any useful task. It helps children understand that computers obey instructions to the letter and are unable to infer meaning or recognise when a result is not intended. Children also learn that computer programmers draw from a limited vocabulary in order to write their programs and only find out the results when they run them. This is why they need to refine them afterwards through the process of debugging. Bugs are not mistakes, rather they are part of the cycle of testing and fixing programs.

This activity is a variation of the jam sandwich algorithm popularised by Philip Bagge, **http://code-it.co.uk/unplugged/jamsandwich**. It has links with Chapter 8: Cooks, which looks at analysing recipes from an algorithmic perspective. The ideas can be related to real-world examples of automated food preparation.

Cross-curricular links

There is a link with instructional writing in English:

- Write clearly, accurately and coherently, adapting their language and style in and for a range of contexts, purposes and audiences.

(DfE, 2013)

Age range

Key Stage 1 or beginning Key Stage 2

Lesson plan

Learning outcomes

To collaborate on creating algorithms for preparing a food snack.

To evaluate the effectiveness of algorithms.

To understand that programming languages have a limited vocabulary.

'I can' statements:

- I can collaborate with others to solve a problem.
- I can decompose a sequence of movements.
- I can persevere in order to find an efficient solution to a problem.
- I can evaluate my algorithm by testing and fixing.
- I can use logical reasoning to debug a program.

Key words and questions

precision, algorithm, instructions, robotics, efficiency, tinkering, sequence, automation, pseudocode

- How can we simplify language in order to produce instructions that robots understand?
- Are shorter or longer instructions more effective?
- How can we make sure a robot makes identical food snacks?
- What happens if the robot runs out of ingredients?

Activities

Time	Teacher activity	Student activity	Resources
10 mins	Discuss what would happen if people followed instructions exactly as they were given. For example: 'play on the computer', 'shake hands with your friend'. Aim to get across the idea that computers can't tell the difference between sensible and ridiculous responses.	Pupils think-pair-share some instructions not to be taken literally, considering what they mean and how a robot might respond to them, e.g. 'get cracking', 'break a leg', 'put a sock in it', 'bite the bullet', 'break the ice', 'butter someone up', go back to the drawing board', 'eat my hat'.	A set of example common sayings.
10 mins	Introduce the idea of programming the teacher to make a food snack. The teacher acts as the robot interpreting instructions literally in a comical way.	Pupils take turns at calling out instructions to control the teacher robot.	Equipment and ingredients to make a food snack,

(Continued)

(Continued)

Time	Teacher activity	Student activity	Resources
	Think about whether it is better to have a large or a small set of instructions. Better for whom?		e.g. toast, a poached egg, a salad, a cup of tea, snack noodles, an ice-cream float, a bowl of cereal, a fruit salad or fruit kebab, a milk shake, a smoothie or a sandwich.
20 mins	Explain that pupils are now going to create their own sets of instructions for making a snack.	Pupils choose a snack. They make a list of the vocabulary that they would need to program a robot to make the snack. They use the vocabulary list to write their own algorithm or part of an algorithm and test it out on each other using role-play.	A list of snacks to choose from, together with some images. Some cooking utensils to assist with the role-play.
15 mins	Discuss the importance of removing bugs by considering some situations where bugs would have enormous consequences such as a rocket launch or a signalling control on a railway. Consider how can we make sure a robot makes identical food snacks and what happens if the robot runs out of ingredients.	Pupils test and fix their algorithms and talk about the process of debugging. Pupils peer assess using a traffic light system and the 'I can' statements as a guide. Pupils relate their activities to real-world situations.	List of 'I can' statements.

Variations, differentiation and extensions

Differentiation

Provide additional support by using an app such as PicCollage to sequence a set of photos before inventing the instructions.

Children could be given the vocabulary that is needed to construct the commands for a particular food snack and then construct their algorithms by joining words together. Here is an example set of words for sandwich making from Phil Bagge **http://code-it. co.uk/wp-content/uploads/2015/05/writesandwichalgorithm2.pdf**.

For those who need an extra challenge you could replace the nouns describing the food, hands and knife with the words 'objects', 'grippers' and 'tools' to replicate instructions to a robot. Decide in advance what commands your robot can understand and then work with a robot who shows confusion through a gesture such as shaking his head or returns an error message. Children could search for some example syntax errors in order to tune into 'robot language' and make their robot's responses more realistic.

Figure 1.4   Using PicCollage to sequence photos

(by Chantelle James)

Table 1.1   A set of vocabulary for instructing a robot to make a sandwich

Right Hand	spread	butter	fast
Left Hand	scoop	tub	repeat
Pick up	packet	bread	hard
Press down	knife	slice	soft
cut	blade	plate	forward
Put down	handle	turn	back
hold	jam	top	put
unscrew	jar	bottom	Table
remove	lid	slow	Surface

Extensions

If the food snack includes some repeated sequences of actions, children could be encouraged to create a stored procedure, which can be called into the program when it is needed. Examples might be procedures describing a set of instructions to 'slice', 'pour' or 'stir'.

Children could also look for opportunities to add if/else conditional statements so that the program contains choices (selection) and do/until loops (iteration). For example:

IF (sugar is required);
THEN add sugar;
ELSE do nothing;
ENDIF;
WHILE (kettle is not full);
DO keep filling kettle;
ENDWHILE;

You might introduce the idea of pseudocode as a way of planning a program before beginning coding by writing a set of instructions in plain English and look at some examples.

Plugged activities

An obvious follow-on activity for all of the unplugged ideas in this chapter is to program some real robots. It is a good idea to think of some real-world examples of robotics in order to bridge the gap between the digital and physical worlds, and to reinforce the relevance of the robotic activities undertaken in school. An example might be to think about rescue robots and the advantages of using a robot or drone in a disaster scenario such as a tsunami or an earthquake. Pupils could create simulated rescue scenes and test their robot's ability to fulfil objectives such as previewing the site or transporting materials to a survivor. They might customise their robots to give them additional features and retest before designing a final rescue robot, which solves the problems they identified. Think about using Autodesk 123D design app for this.

Success criteria and assessment

- All children will produce a set of instructions.

- Most children will debug their algorithm and explain why it is better.

- Some children will write a bug-free algorithm.

- Some children will use procedures, repetition and selection in their algorithms.

Assessment for learning techniques such as open questioning can be used during the starter and plenary in order to identify prior knowledge and to identify gaps and next steps for learning. Encourage children to continue to ask 'why' and 'how' questions while they are working together. You can use the 'I can' statements together with a 'traffic light' system for evaluating individual pupils' progress, and children themselves can self or peer assess against these. Children's vocabulary sets will provide evidence for summative assessment against the learning objectives and could be added to a profile of achievement in computing.

Reflective questions

- Why is it important for pupils to think carefully about the kind of language they use when creating sequences of instructions for robots?

- How would you introduce the concept of debugging to your pupils?

- How can you encourage pupils to solve computing problems independently?

- What do you think is the value of giving pupils real-world examples of robotics?

Discussion

Algorithms and programs

The key word in this chapter is 'algorithm' – a defined set of operations that completes a task. In other words, a set of instructions. But we also talk about 'programming' and 'coding', often synonymously.

What's the difference between a 'program' and an 'algorithm'? The algorithm is the set of instructions that the person (or computer) will carry out. The program is just the precise way it's written. For instance, using the notation from Activity 1, here are four programs that students might have come up with:

Each of these *programs* is different, but they all express the same *algorithm*: take five steps forward. Programmers use different programming languages because each programming language makes some things easy and some things hard, but the algorithms they use are the same in all the different languages. You can treat 'coding' just as a pure synonym for 'programming' and 'code' as a synonym for 'program'.

Because the algorithms remain the same even if the programs change, computer scientists are much more interested in algorithms than programs, and the computational thinking skill being addressed in this chapter is algorithms, not programs.

Each of the activities in this chapter is about defining, testing and debugging algorithms. The details of the programs used to instantiate the algorithm do not really matter.

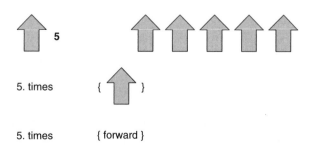

Figure 1.5   Four ways of expressing an algorithm

The first 'computers', dating back to the seventeenth century, were people who carried out defined calculations for various purposes, often compiling tables of calculated numbers for seafaring navigators. In 1936, Alan Turing defined what we now think of as 'computation' by defining the Turing Machine, the conceptual basis for all modern digital computers. He defined the Turing Machine as the abstraction of what a human computer would need: a precise set of instructions, the ability to remember their current instruction, and a notepad, pencil, and rubber for recording intermediate results.

Logic and control

The simplest algorithms are just sequences of operations, much like the instructions in a cooking recipe: do this, then do that, then do the other, and you end up with some yummy biscuits.

When children are first understanding algorithms, this idea of breaking down a process into a series of steps, each of which is well defined, and following them methodically, is enough of a challenge for them.

Sequences of steps alone can only get you so far, though. More complex tasks demand more complex algorithms, including repetition of some instructions and selection of one group of instructions or another. With just these three constructs (sequence, selection, repetition) you can describe any algorithm that exists.

Precision and abstraction

Algorithms are described as collections of operations that are carried out in a methodical process. A good deal of computational thinking is about how to structure those operations to achieve the desired outcome. But that raises the question of how those operations come about. There's nothing inherently right about making people navigate an obstacle course by giving instructions at the level of 'move forward' and 'climb over'. How would these operations apply if the task were extended to an 'obstacle' where someone had to walk without stepping on the cracks in the pavement?

Students might think about how to program a person with a different set of 'primitive' operations. Robots are really, *really* stupid and have to be taught what their limbs are and how to move them, let alone how to take a step or kick a ball. Search YouTube for videos on 'Darpa robotics challenge fail' (**www.youtube.com/watch?v=g0TaYhjpOfo**) and 'robocup fail' (**www.youtube.com/watch?v=j9arXtrhZBo**) for robots that have forgotten how to stand or walk. You could compare this to how babies have to learn to walk and talk.

The same thing applies to programming languages. 'High level' languages make some things easy by having basic operations that are well suited to a particular application, while 'low level' languages are often more flexible but require longer programs.

Scratch is very good at making animations or simple games; equivalent programs in Python are often longer, but Python is more flexible than Scratch.

Summary and Key Points

In this chapter we have used the analogy of robots in order to help children to learn how to think computationally. We have focused on the skills of writing precise algorithms and debugging them to make them more efficient.

- Algorithms are precisely defined sets of instructions for performing a particular task.
- An algorithm can be performed by anything (computer or person) that can interpret the instructions and perform the actions they call for.
- Some algorithms are just sequences of steps, one after the other.
- More complex algorithms use conditional statements (IF-THEN-ELSE) and repetition (FOR, WHILE, REPEAT-UNTIL).
- It is normal for programmers to make mistakes and debugging code is an important part of the programming process.

Resources and further reading

The Barefoot Programme – supporting teachers with computer science
http://barefootcas.org.uk

CAS computational thinking – A Guide for teachers
http://community.computingatschool.org.uk/resources/2324

Computational Thinking teacher resources from the International Society for Technology in Education (ISTE) and the Computer Science Teachers Association (CSTA)
https://csta.acm.org/Curriculum/sub/CurrFiles/472.11CTTeacherResources_2ed-SP-vF.pdf

Computing resources produced by Phil Bagge
http://code-it.co.uk

Computer science fundamentals for elementary school from Code.org
https://code.org/educate/curriculum/elementary-school

References

Allsop, Y and Sedman, B (2015) *Primary Computing in Action.* Woodbridge: John Catt.

Bird, J, Caldwell, H and Mayne, P (eds) (2014) *Lessons in Teaching Computing in Primary Schools.* London: Learning Matters/SAGE.

Caldwell, H and Bird, J (eds) (2015) *Teaching with Tablets.* London: Learning Matters/SAGE.

Curzon, P, Dorling, M, Ng, T, Selby, C and Woollard, J (2014) *Developing Computational Thinking in the Classroom: a Framework.* Swindon: Computing at School.

Curzon, P, McOwan, PW, Plant, N and Meagher, LR (2014, November) Introducing teachers to computational thinking using unplugged storytelling. In *Proceedings of the 9th Workshop in Primary and Secondary Computing Education* (89–92). ACM.

Department for Education (DfE) (2011) *Teachers' Standards*. Available from **https://www.gov.uk/ government/uploads/system/uploads/attachment_data/file/283566/Teachers_standard_ information.pdf** (accessed 23 December 2015).

National Curriculum in England: *Computing programmes of study, Department for Education* (11 September 2013).

National Curriculum in England: *English programmes of study—key stages 1 and 2*, Department for Education (16 July 2014).

Selby, C, Dorling, M and Woollard, J (2014) Evidence of assessing computational thinking. *Author's original* (1–11).

Chapter 2

MUSICIANS

I would teach children music, physics, and philosophy; but most importantly music, for the patterns in music and all the arts are the keys to learning.

Plato

Introduction

Music is something that everyone can relate to and everyone is exposed to. Whether it is someone tapping their foot on a bus, listening to the radio in the car or singing favourite nursery rhymes at school, music is inescapable. Beyond this, music allows people to express their thoughts and feelings, and identify with each other in a different way. Capturing this as a teaching concept is not a new idea. However, rather than just sharing learning experiences through music or using music to enhance the atmosphere of a classroom, we will explore using music as the root of teaching computing concepts while reaping the benefits of increased engagement and a less formal atmosphere.

Listening to musical compositions causes a variety of areas of the brain to engage and react (Alluri *et al.*, 2012). This effect is even stronger if the individual is creating the music through using an instrument and can cause long-term changes in how the brain works (Gaser and Schlaug, 2003). Making use of the power of music to benefit learning, this chapter builds on the complex nature of music by breaking it down to its core components such as repetition, singling out the different strands involved such as a bass beat or a melody, and recognising each interaction throughout a composition. All of this allows us to explore key computing concepts in a context that is familiar to all of us.

This chapter will explore how we can develop pupils' logical reasoning and problem-solving skills in the context of musical activities. Three activities are presented:

- *Just dance*: learning about pattern recognition, decomposition and repetition by analysing and recreating popular dance routines.

- *Human beatbox:* learning about repetition and parallelism by building a song using the different sounds that children can make using just their bodies!

- *Music maker:* learning about decomposition and abstraction by taking a song and reducing it to its bare bones.

Learning Outcomes

At the end of this chapter you should be able to:

- understand the wider benefits of learning computing through music;
- recognise how core computing concepts might be presented in a musical context;
- understand how to use music to teach computational thinking.

Links to Teachers' Standards

Working through this chapter will help you meet The following Teachers' Standards are particularly relevant to this chapter:

TS1 Set high expectations which inspire, motivate and challenge pupils.
TS3 Demonstrate good subject and curriculum knowledge.
TS4 Plan and teach well structured lessons.

(DfE, 2011)

Unplugged Activity 1: Just dance

Overview

Children watch each other perform well-known dance routines, looking at each move carefully and recognising patterns that repeat. They think about how to record the routine so that it can be used as a set of instructions for someone else, and they finally create an algorithm, which decomposes the full dance routine into smaller steps.

Computational thinking features developed

When children complete this activity, they will record their creation as an *algorithm*. They will use their skills of *pattern recognition* to find similarities and *repetition* within the dance routine allowing them to think carefully about how the dance was created. This is a process of *decomposition*, which focuses on combining simple movements to create a finished piece. Each test of the algorithm allows for a simple, and very visual, way to *debug* and ensure that the end result matches the original stimulus.

Cross-curricular links

PE

Key Stage 1:

- Perform dances using simple movement patterns.

- Master basic movements including co-ordination, and begin to apply these in a range of activities.

Key Stage 2:

- Perform dances using a range of movement patterns.

- Compare their performances with previous ones and demonstrate improvement to achieve their personal best.

Age range

This activity and dance combination, the 'Hokey Cokey', is suitable for Key Stage 1 children, but the activity is easily adapted for different ages and abilities.

Other popular children's songs such as 'Heads, Shoulders, Knees and Toes' or 'Wind the Bobbin Up' are suitable for Key Stage 1. Lower Key Stage 2 children could use familiar party songs (e.g. Los del Rio: Macarena; Steps: 5, 6, 7, 8; Whigfield: Saturday Night). Upper Key Stage 2 children might be more engaged with contemporary pop songs, as long as the lyrics and dance moves are appropriate for school.

Lesson plan

Learning objectives

Computational thinking

- to decompose a problem into its parts
- to recognise patterns and use repetitions to demonstrate this

Computing

- to write a precise algorithm
- to create and debug a simple program

PE

- to use simple movement patterns

Key words and questions

algorithms – a set of instructions that run in sequence

decomposition – breaking a problem down into small steps

repetition – to use a loop in a program

- Which action comes first?

- Are there times where we do an action more than once?

- Can you put these actions in order?

- What's the next instruction? After we've done x we need to do what?

Activities

What will the students be doing at different stages through the lesson?

Time	Teacher activity	Student activity	Resources
5 mins	Lead the song 'Hokey Cokey', modelling the actions.	Pupils sing/dance along.	
5 mins	Introduce the idea of recording the instructions for the actions as a set of pictures. Ask which action comes first and then model it. Children take a photo.	Share with the class which action comes first.	iPad or tablet to take and share photos of actions. If technology is limited, children could draw stick figures of the actions.

Time	Teacher activity	Student activity	Resources
15 mins	Highlight mistakes but leave them to debug as a group.	Children take photos of all the actions for the 'right arm' sequence, repeatedly checking the song to ensure completeness.	
10 mins	Go through the actions for right arm and check they're in the correct order by singing the song together.	Once complete, children share the photos that they have taken with the class.	
5 mins	Model adding a loop with an arrow going back to the top and including a 'left arm' photo. Ask children if there are any other times we would need to repeat a section of the 'Hokey Cokey', e.g. in, out, in out.	In groups, children sequence the action photos using a camera roll, book creator app, or similar. Children debug their algorithm.	
10 mins		Children discuss how they should record the next part of the song. They add loops throughout their algorithm using the sequenced photos and drawing in the arrows to show the 'flow'.	
5 mins		Children share their algorithm with another group who point to each step when the children sing the next bit.	

Success criteria and assessment

If pupils have met the learning outcomes, they will:

- have broken the dance into smaller parts (decomposition);
- have identified repetition in the dance routine;
- have visually shown the sequence of instructions (algorithm).

The children's understanding should be checked through questioning and asking them to talk through their algorithms, showing you which parts match each section of the dance. The children's flowcharts will also allow insights into pupils' understanding of how to decompose a larger idea and which sections need to be repeated.

Scope for differentiation and extension

Support

Take into consideration that if any of the children in the class don't know the song, then the task will be more difficult. With this in mind, aim to have a device where the children can easily watch other sections of the dance and play it back as necessary.

Using recording options makes this lesson accessible to a wide range of children with SEN and EAL. Alternative ways of recording such as using photos within an app such as 'PicCollage' could increase the accessibility.

Stretch

To stretch those children who are confident, choose a different song to the one you have modelled and give the children some completed algorithms with mistakes in them. The children must then systematically and carefully work through each step of the algorithm to debug any mistakes.

Unplugged Activity 2: Human beatbox

Overview

In this activity children use their bodies and voices to create a piece of music from a combination of rhythmic beats. As they add each sound to their mix they develop their own algorithm for the music, making use of repetition to ensure consistency. The activity ends with a discussion about simultaneously running several threads (parallelism) and how we can use these to build up to our own musical creations. The computing concept of parallelism is based on the idea of dividing large problems into smaller ones, which are then solved at the same time.

The lack of language in this activity makes it accessible to children who struggle with reading or speaking English. This can make it a good lesson for assessing understanding of concepts without other barriers to learning such as language and literacy level.

Computational thinking features developed

Children will record their creation as an *algorithm* for recreating the music. Music features much *repetition*, including using an intuitive use of *nested loops* (*a loop within a loop*) for different, but synchronised, beats. This introduces the concept of *parallelism* as we are controlling several separate sets of instructions at the same time.

Cross-curricular links

Music
Key Stage 1:

- Use their voices expressively and creatively by singing songs and speaking chants and rhymes.

- Play tuned and untuned instruments musically.

- Experiment with, create, select and combine sounds using the interrelated dimensions of music.

Key Stage 2:

- Play and perform in solo and ensemble contexts, using their voices and playing musical instruments with increasing accuracy, fluency, control and expression.

- Improvise and compose music for a range of purposes using the interrelated dimensions of music.

Age range

This activity and dance combination is suitable for late Key Stage 2 children. Earlier Key Stage 2 children may need support identifying different beats in songs. You could start Key Stage 1 children with simple clapping that is built up with layers.

Lesson plan

Learning objectives

Computational thinking

- to use nested loops within in algorithm
- to recognise the use of parallelism

Computing

- to design a program that accomplishes a specific goal
- working towards using sequence, repetition and variables in programs

Music

- to compose music with fluency, accuracy and control
- to perform as part of an ensemble

Key words and questions

algorithms – a set of instructions that run in sequence

nested loops – loops, or repeated sections, that are working inside another loop

parallelism – running several different sets of instructions at the same time

- What order does a computer run instructions in?

- How do we know which instructions will go next?

- What *ingredients* do we need to create a good song?

- What instructions can we give to start our code?

- How do the people who are playing instruments know to begin playing?

Activities

What will the students be doing at different stages through the lesson?

Time	Teacher activity	Student activity	Resources
5 mins	Clapping a rhythm which the class copies. Progressively make it more complicated.	Pupils copy the rhythms.	
10 mins	Then split the class into two groups, each doing a different (but simple) pattern. Repeat with different rhythms and groups.	Pupils discuss with partners how they can depict what they've been doing as an algorithm.	
5 mins	After everyone is confident, ask the children how they could record this as an algorithm.		Large sheets of paper for drawing flowcharts.
10 mins	Show the webtool 'Incredibox' to illustrate how this approach can be built up. (**www.incredibox.com**)	Children write the algorithm for a basic clapping rhythm and share examples.	Model flowcharts, if necessary.
5 mins	Plenary: ask children how to represent simultaneous playing with a single-threaded flowchart. Lead the discussion towards parallelism and co-ordinating the start of different threads. Use the analogy of an orchestral conductor.		
10 mins		In groups, children build on their initial clapping algorithm with other combinations of sounds. Encourage them to start with only one additional beat – once that one is sorted, add another, and so on. Children continue to develop their algorithm in groups, including triggers for people starting. Children share their algorithms with the class, perhaps sticking the sheets on the wall.	Video or photo of orchestral conductor. Use a visualiser to share the algorithm and not just the musical outcome with the class.

Success criteria and assessment

If pupils have met the learning outcomes, they will:

- have written an algorithm using repetition including nested loops;
- have increased the complexity of their algorithm by running more than one algorithm at once;
- have explained the necessity to use parallelism in the algorithm;
- have written broadcast messages within their algorithm to instruct other parts when to start.

Questioning can be used to ensure that pupils understand the concepts behind what they are doing.

The flowcharts allow insights into who understands which parts of the algorithm need to be repeated (and for how long) and when and how different threads are triggered.

Scope for differentiation and extension

Support

Children with dyslexia may find it difficult to maintain a rhythm and sequence. Multisensory teaching styles may help: modelling the rhythm and letting the pupil copy (auditory), showing the steps in the algorithm while modelling the rhythm (connecting visual and auditory), and tapping, touching or throwing a beanbag in that pattern (kinaesthetic).

If children are struggling with sequencing or parallelism, encourage them to act out their algorithm with actions in addition to, or instead of, sounds. This develops the *debugging*, *persevering* and *collaborating* approaches to computational thinking.

Stretch

More able students can be challenged by asking them to model a more complex (perhaps a commercial) song, identifying where the repetition changes or stops. Perhaps the bridge section of the song breaks the repetition temporarily before it returns for the chorus, or the rhythm stays the same but the instrument or key changes

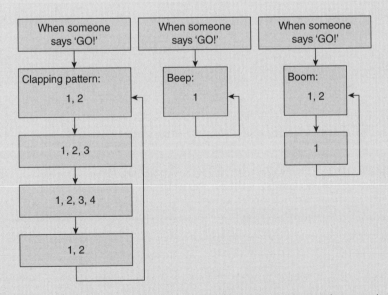

Figure 2.1 The Human Beatbox: algorithm for three people's roles starting at the same time

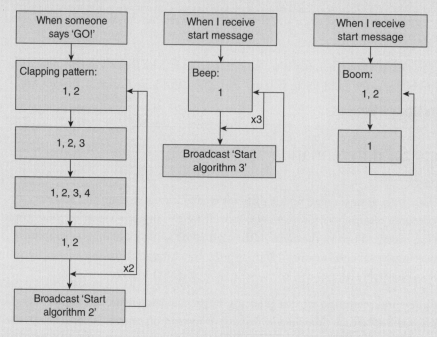

Figure 2.2 The algorithm for three people's roles running parallel and starting each algorithm at a different time

for a section before returning to the original pattern. Creating algorithms with these kind of variations show a deep understanding of the concepts as they have to build in differences that do not run infinitely.

Unplugged Activity 3: Music maker

Overview

Popular songs are often rather repetitive at many levels such as verse-chorus, lyrics or musical phrases. Identifying these repeated parts and drawing flowcharts of songs can help children understand the ideas of repetition and abstraction within computing. Children can then use their own algorithm for the song to create a personal version with just a few changes to the content of their algorithm.

Computational thinking features developed

This activity requires pupils to listen carefully to a piece of music and use *pattern recognition* to identify *repetition*. They then represent this structure in a flowchart that uses loops to show repeated sections at different levels. This is extended by the use of *abstraction* as the pupils identify which parts of the song are fixed and which can be changed without affecting the overall song. The lesson culminates in using these skills to create their own song *algorithm*, which can then be used by the children when making their own version of the song.

Cross-curricular links

Music

Key Stage 1:

- Use their voices expressively and creatively by singing songs and speaking chants and rhymes.

- Listen with concentration and understanding to a range of high-quality live and recorded music.

Key Stage 2:

- Listen with attention to detail and recall sounds with increasing aural memory.

- Appreciate and understand a wide range of high-quality live and recorded music drawn from different traditions and from great composers and musicians.

Age range

The song used in this sample, 'I am the Music Man', is suitable for early Key Stage 2. Simpler songs such as 'Twinkle Twinkle' or 'Old MacDonald' can be used with younger children. Older children might prefer to analyse current pop songs, so long as there is a clear, repetitive structure. All children, especially EAL children, benefit from using familiar songs.

Lesson plan

Learning objectives

Computational thinking

- to use pattern recognition to decompose a song
- to understand the benefits of abstraction

Computing

- to use logical reasoning to explain how some simple algorithms work
- (working towards) to use sequence, repetition and variables in programs

Music

- to listen with attention and detail
- to consider how songs are composed

Key words and questions

pattern recognition – spotting and making use of similarities

decomposition – breaking a problem into small pieces

abstraction – removing unnecessary detail

- What *ingredients* do we need to create a good song?

- Which parts of the song can you hear more than once?

- Do we need to write the same things every time? What could we do instead?

- How could we make this simpler?

- Is it going to be the same every time?

Activities

What will the students be doing at different stages through the lesson?

Time	Teacher activity	Student activity	Resources
10 mins	Play pupils the song and ask them to listen carefully for patterns. Give children a copy of the lyrics. Ask them to represent the lyrics in a flowchart.	Children make notes (or think about) repeated words, lines and motifs in the song.	Recording of the song. Printed lyric sheets. Large sheets of paper for making flowcharts. Model flowchart for a different song if this approach is unfamiliar to children.
10 mins	Introduce the concept of abstraction and simplicity, asking them to note repetition in the song with arrows making loops. (Figure 2.1)	Children create a flow chart by cutting up the lyrics and arranging them on their tables, drawing in repetition as needed.	Show children an example of the algorithm not repeated because the one word of the instrument changes each time.
15 mins	Prompt children to notice repeated structures even if the detail (words) are different (e.g. different verses follow the same pattern). (Figure 2.2)	Children consider how to remove the words from the song and store them elsewhere, perhaps a list at the side. Children amend their flowchart.	
20 mins	Explain that the children have created an algorithm for the song. Model how the song can be adapted by changing just some parts. For instance, 'I am the builder man, I come from far away and I can use…' and then change the list to tools.	Children sing along the amended song with the tools they listed as a class. Can they think of any other versions that would work?	Show a completed flowchart (algorithm) and edit to show how easily it can be changed.
5 mins		Children spend 5 minutes coming up with their own versions and sharing them with their partners.	

Success criteria and assessment

If pupils have met the learning outcomes, they will:

- have separated the song into sections;

- have shown the sequence of instructions using a flowchart;

- have shown which parts are repeated and how many times;
- have separated lists of items from the main instructions (reducing the song to its simplest form);
- have an algorithm for the song that can be used to know the song's lyrics;
- be able to create their own version by changing just a few words.

Questioning can be used to ensure that pupils understand the concepts behind the activity, such as the advantages of terseness or succinctness, and the adaptability or reusability of abstracted algorithms. The flowcharts will indicate which pupils understand repetition and how it requires control (e.g. the number of times to repeat a section).

Scope for differentiation and extension

Support

Children may struggle with modelling the whole song at once. You may help them by focusing first on just the chorus, or the chorus and first verse, then adding other sections as the children develop their flowcharts.

Stretch

If children are able easily to identify repetition, you may prompt them for ways to abstract away the repeated instances of the chorus, instead bundling them in a procedure that can be called from the main song (see Figure 2.4).

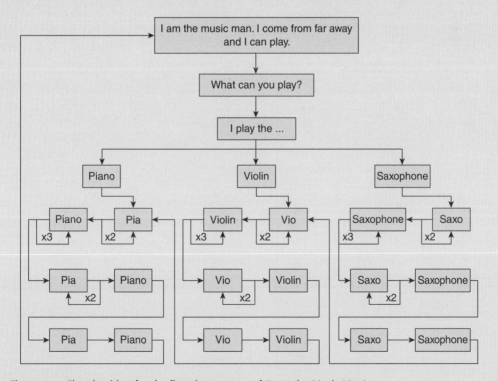

Figure 2.3   The algorithm for the first three verses of 'I am the Music Man'

You could ask children listen to the instruments, paying attention to repeated phrases and different beats. This is a natural lead into the 'human beatbox' activity below.

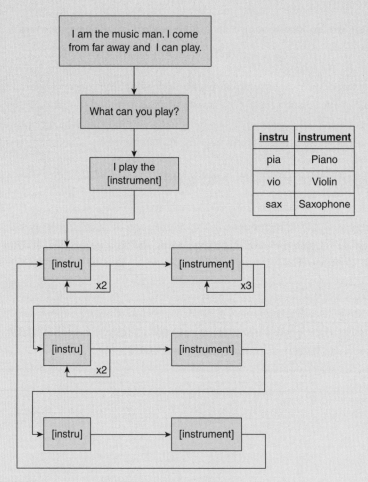

Figure 2.4 The *abstracted* algorithm for 'I am the Music Man'

Reflective questions

- Think about the learners in your class: who might benefit from using music to engage them?

- What other everyday tasks are examples of repetition?

- How could you combine teaching a musical concept, such as rounds, while reinforcing the musical concept of computational thinking?

- What can you do to ensure the concept is understood in relation to the computing context it will ultimately be used in?

Discussion

The benefits of music education are well recognised. From increasing the development of visual and auditory memory (Degé et al., 2011), to significant improvements in the development of verbal memory (Ho et al., 2003) and increased reading ability and better vocabulary in their native language (Kraus and Chandrasekaran, 2010), comprehensive music education can open many doors. Using music as a medium to teach other concepts is not unique, and has even been tried and tested as a pedagogy in subjects such as economics (Tinari and Khandke, 2000), but in this instance we are teaching key concepts which are applicable in two subjects: music and computing.

Music is universally accessible to everyone and is a great motivator; who doesn't have a special memory tied to a specific song? With this in mind, using music in a computing lesson can reach out to a group of pupils who may otherwise have decided that computing is not for them. An unplugged approach to teaching computing through music breaks down barriers of accessibility and inhibits the 'It never works when I use it!' comments. Beyond this, music also empowers children to see the world differently and to recognise that there isn't always a 'right' or 'wrong' but instead there are just 'different' ways of doing something.

Creative computing

There is a common misconception in the world that computing is not a creative subject. This stems from the understanding that computers have to follow rules and as such are restrictive and unable to enhance creativity. McCormack and d'Inverno (2012) explore the notion that computers themselves may or may not be capable of creativity independent of a user; however, they argue that there is general consensus among those who work with computers that computers can inspire and promote creativity in their human users.

Ask anyone who's had to fix a computer bug, or ascertain why a network isn't working, and they will explain that you need to get creative. In fact, the *Oxford Dictionary's* definition of creativity – *the use of imagination or original ideas to create something; inventiveness* – is what technology and computing is all about: making and inventing (**www.oxforddictionaries.com/definition/english/creativity** accessed 30.3.16).

This could be inventing technology and hardware or, more likely, inventing solutions to problems through developing software. Either way, computing is creative and digital making is emphasised in the computing curriculum.

Nevertheless, it can be hard to help pupils recognise the connection between computing and creativity, so making the connection with music is a great way to start unifying these ideas. Educationally, linking what children find entertaining and enjoy, such as engaging with music, also increases their immersion with the content being conveyed. This has been illustrated previously through video games where Barab *et al*. (2010) used the connections with children's entertainment to successfully create opportunities for learning.

Pedagogy

Whenever you are teaching a computing lesson there is always an amount of time wasted at the start due to retrieving the computers or walking to the computer suite, then logging on and getting the equipment sorted for the main part of the lesson. This is unavoidable and necessary; however, using unplugged lesson ideas means that you can get straight to the computing learning without the hassle or even while the computers are loading. This means that you can rest assured that the technology won't let you down and you can focus your energy on teaching the crucial concept to the class rather than as tech support (Bell *et al*., 2012). As well as this, Bell *et al*. (2012) go on to explain that the lack of technology reduces student distractions and prevents them from blaming the device for their own mistakes. Wing (2008, p3721) sums this up nicely by stating *we do not want the tool to get in the way of understanding the concepts*.

Thinking beyond the benefits to classroom management, unplugged activities are inherently kinaesthetic, which means that they can appeal to a wider range of learners who may not find it easy to read code. Bell and Newton suggest that while the children approach these activities themselves, the teacher should step back and allow them to explore independently (Bell and Newton, 2013). The lessons discussed here are self-explanatory; children will know when their musical algorithm is incorrect and so take the time to scaffold their learning through careful use of questioning. This allows children time to construct their own understanding and solutions, and ultimately test the robustness of their understanding of the key concepts.

Barab *et al*. (2010) suggest a theory of learning called 'Transformational Play' which explores the use of first person computer games where the user has to make decisions on behalf of a character, as a method of teaching concepts and seeing learners apply them to real-life situations. They found that engagement, as in just playing a video game, was not enough to ensure transformational play. Instead, the play had to involve taking the role of the main character, applying conceptual understanding and making choices that affected the game. In this way users made a difference to the game by using their knowledge to help solve a socially significant problem. The principles of this theory also apply to the lessons we have outlined here. Children take on the main role of creating the music; they use their conceptual understanding of repetition; their choices affect the music which they create and ultimately they address the socially significant problem of what to share with the class at the end. This more informal and personal approach to learning makes the concepts much more accessible and appealing to children.

When considering unplugged activities as a way of teaching a computational thinking concept, it is important to consider when in the teaching cycle they would be most appropriate. For trickier concepts, I would spend an entire lesson preceding the one where I wished the children to use the concept ensuring they have a thorough understanding of the concept. However, if you have previously introduced the concept and are just reminding the children, then it may be appropriate for a quick starter activity while the computers are logging on (Bell and Newton, 2013). Alternatively, it is worth considering the use of a carefully chosen unplugged activity as a plenary. Can the children use the concept in a different context? What about teaching the dance activity above and challenging the children to spot the repetition in a song at the end of the session? This can provide a great assessment opportunity as you can quickly see those who have quite a narrow understanding of the concept and identify those who understand it more confidently.

Concept: Repetition – what do they need to know?

The use of repetition in programming is one of the key programming principles that children need to understand, and although it is only included explicitly in the Key Stage 2 curriculum, understanding the basic concept that you can run a program, or part of a program, more than once at Key Stage 1 will allow children to 'create and debug simple programs' successfully. In programming, the process of repetition is referred to as using a 'loop' and the main motivation for programmers to use a loop is for the programmer to be more efficient and reduce the likelihood of human error from writing more code than is necessary.

In essence, there are two different types of loops in programming: 'while' and 'for'. 'While loops' continue until a condition is met, for example, 'until the sprite touches a certain colour'. 'For loops' repeat for a predetermined number of times, for example, 'do x 4'. Thinking about these concepts in the context of music and dance, you might repeat a certain dance move while the chorus is playing. This can be useful as we may not know how many times we can fit in that move during the chorus. On the other hand, we might repeat the line of a song we are singing four times before moving on to the next verse. This would use a 'for loop'.

When using a 'while loop' the program is checking a 'Boolean' condition, whether something is True or False. The answer to 'is the sprite touching red?' is always going to be either true or false. Equally, we can use mathematical statements like 'loop while score < 10' where 'score' is a variable. Once again, whether or not the score is less than 10 it is going to give a True or False answer. This 'while loop' can be utilised to make something repeat forever by saying 'repeat while x True' where it is never going to be changed to false. This is called an infinite loop and is executed continuously until the program is terminated. In our music context, you may want the bass beat to repeat the same backing beat continually from the beginning to the end so that you can add variety with the melody.

Finally, most programs will not only use loops they will also use nested loops. This is where you have one loop inside another. Unplugged activities can illustrate how something that seems complicated on-screen can be simply shared as a concept. In Activity 3 in this chapter, we are repeating the verses for 'I am the Music Man'; this is repeated while there are still more verses to play. Within this, we are repeating words for the song, for example 'pia, pia' before 'piano' for the number of times as works in the song. This is a nested loop.

When using nested loops, it is really important to separate out the code so as to see which bits are looping where. In text-based programming languages, this is done using indents to align anything within one loop. In Scratch, this is done with the coloured arm wrapping around the code. When teaching this concept unplugged I recommend colour-coding different sections so that it is really clear to children what is repeated and where.

Transference

Using music to introduce key concepts such as repetition and parallelism is a great way to enthuse children about topics that may seem to have very little relevance to them otherwise (Settle et al., 2012). Learning through the discipline of music also ensures not just the learning of knowledge (the computing concept) but also that the concept is a skill which children can transfer and use again (Saavedra and Opfer, 2012). For this to happen, however, the links between music and computing need to be made explicit to the class in order for the learning to be most effective (Bell and Newton, 2013). This can be as simple as demonstrating the use of repetition on the computer alongside introducing the unplugged activity. For example, you could show children a video of traffic lights and ask what would happen if these ran once and then stopped. Using an example like this allows children to see the application of the concept, immediately grounding the topic with a practical usage before they begin to construct their own understanding of how to use the concept in their algorithm. Referring back to Wing's (2008) tool analogy, when the children then progress to applying the knowledge on the computer, the tool (the computer) is reinforcing the concept of which they already have a thorough understanding.

Assessment and progression

Measuring the development of computational thinking skills can be difficult as progress occurs in small increments but the skills should be used across the curriculum to ensure all-round understanding (Settle *et al.*, 2012). What should be noticeable, however, is the improvements in children's proficiency at creating more complex programs, including the concepts which you have addressed through the unplugged activities. Therefore, the children's understanding should be assessed through creating open-ended projects which allow the children to apply the concepts that they have been learning (Brennan and Resnick, 2012). Considering our music context, could the children plan their own song modelling the repetition that they have identified in existing songs?

One of the best ways to check a child's understanding of a concept is to ask them to apply it in other instances. For example, once pupils have considered parallelism in a musical context, can they then apply it to other processes? What about when making a layered cake with icing: which processes can be done in parallel and how many people can be usefully involved? This not only applies in unplugged contexts, but also when the children transition to on-screen coding. If a child understands something at a conceptual level, then they can apply it to any other programming language. For example, loops as a concept are in every programming language from Pro-bot, to Lego Wedo, to Scratch, to Python or Java. If you know when and how to use them, then you just need to check the syntax to be able to use them in any language (Repenning *et al.*, 2010).

Capturing the process and checking the children's understanding can happen in many different ways. From the example activities above, you can see examples of the children recording their conceptual understanding through algorithmic flowcharts. However, this may not work for all learners, particularly those who find organisation difficult. Other ways of capturing the process and checking the underlying concepts are understood, rather than just the outcome being achieved, could involve children commenting upon their code or creating a notebook to document thoughts and ideas, recording a screencast discussing what they have included and why, or creating a presentation of their experiences (Brennan and Resnick, 2012).

Support and challenge

The role of the teacher in scaffolding the child's understanding of the concept is crucial. The teacher must guide the children through the activities in order to allow them to discover the solution for themselves. Part of this process involves the children recognising that time spent working on an algorithm which does not work is not time spent wasted, but instead is developing their understanding of a concept to be used in future situations (Bell and Newton, 2013). This needs to be carefully managed by the teacher to ensure the support offered is most useful. For example, children may have common ideas about features they want to include in their programs, such as a score on a game. They may understand the feature, but they often lack the concepts such as an understanding of data and variables. If you are working within Scratch you will need to provide support by highlighting the blocks that will be useful as well as the concepts behind them (Brennan and Resnick, 2012).

When supporting children in their understanding of key computing concepts, making it clear that the expectation is a process rather than an outcome is crucial. Offering support will most likely come from your questioning, asking them to tell you what they have done and suggesting they check through a certain part of their algorithm with their partner. Another way of supporting learners may be to give them part of the algorithm for them to continue or giving them an algorithm that doesn't work for them to fix. This can be less daunting than a blank page but still allows for children to discover and construct the learning for themselves.

As for challenge, one of the main reasons that professional women reported enjoying computing was *the sense of accomplishment that comes from solving the problem* (Almstrum, 2003, p52). This highlights the benefits of a problem-solving approach to computing. The open-ended nature of our unplugged tasks allows children the freedom to pursue their own challenges, not only by being able to solve the conceptual challenge that you have set them but by also allowing them to demonstrate their understanding in other contexts.

Summary and Key Points

The activities outlined above show teachers how music can be a great way to teach accessible and engaging computing concepts. They all are appropriate from Key Stage 1 through to Key Stage 2 with some minor tweaks, and they aim to inspire teachers to use music across the curriculum. By using music, the focus shifts from technology being omnipotent to children thinking about their creative choices.

This chapter specifically focuses on the computational thinking concept of repetition, including the different types of loops and the purpose of these in programming. It aims to show that music can illustrate computational thinking concepts. Each concept is explained in relation to what it is, how it is seen in music and its relation to the context of programming so as to allow for simple transference of knowledge from one context to the other.

Beyond this, computational thinking concepts such as abstraction, parallelism, decomposition and debugging are also shown to have clear links with music, allowing for the consolidation of other concepts while introducing new ones. This allows for the development of conceptual knowledge across a range of skills which can then be applied in an on-screen context.

Finally, the pedagogical choices of how to make the unplugged music-based concept have the greatest impact online are considered alongside the theories of transformational play, constructivist learning and effective transference. The need to choose the amount of time spent on the concept and when to introduce the concept to best benefit learners is also discussed.

Resources and further reading

Incredibox is a beatbox-making website.
www.incredibox.com/v4/

Music Research Institute – a place with lots of information about the benefits of music.
www.mri.ac.uk

Sonic Pi is a way of programming music which can link nicely with the transition from the concept to using it in a computer-based context.
http://sonic-pi.net/

TED Ed: How playing an instrument benefits your brain.
http://ed.ted.com/lessons/how-playing-an-instrument-benefits-your-brain-anita-collins

References

Alluri, V, Toiviainen, P, Jääskeläinen, IP, Glerean, E, Sams, M and Brattico, E (2012) Large-scale brain networks emerge from dynamic processing of musical timbre, key and rhythm. *Neuroimage*, 59(4), 3677–3689.

Almstrum, VL (2003) What is the attraction to computing? *Communications of the ACM*, 46(9), 51–55.

Barab, SA, Gresalfi, M and Ingram-Goble, A (2010) Transformational play: Using games to position person, content, and context. *Educational Researcher*, 39(7), 525–536.

Bell, T and Newton, H (2013) Using Computer Science Unplugged as a Teaching Tool. Distributed under a Creative Commons Attribution-NonCommercial-NoDerivatives license.

Bell, T, Rosamond, F and Casey, N (2012) Computer science unplugged and related projects in math and computer science popularization. In Bodlaender, HL, Downey, R, Fomin, FV, Marx, D. *The Multivariate Algorithmic Revolution and Beyond* (pp. 398–456). Berlin/Heidelberg: Springer.

Brennan, K and Resnick, M (2012, April) New frameworks for studying and assessing the development of computational thinking. In *Proceedings of the 2012 annual meeting of the American Educational Research Association*, Vancouver, Canada.

Degé, F, Wehrum, S, Stark, R and Schwarzer, G (2011) The influence of two years of school music training in secondary school on visual and auditory memory. *European Journal of Developmental Psychology*, 8(5), 608–623.

Department for Education (DfE) (2011) *Teachers' Standards*. Available from **www.gov.uk/government/uploads/system/uploads/attachment_data/file/283566/Teachers_standard_information.pdf** (accessed 23 December 2015).

Gaser, C and Schlaug, G (2003) Brain structures differ between musicians and non-musicians. *The Journal of Neuroscience*, 23(27), 9240–9245.

Ho, YC, Cheung, MC and Chan, AS (2003) Music training improves verbal but not visual memory: Cross-sectional and longitudinal explorations in children. *Neuropsychology*, 17(3), 439.

Kraus, N and Chandrasekaran, B (2010) Music training for the development of auditory skills. *Nature Reviews Neuroscience*, 11(8), 599–605.

McCormack, J and d'Inverno, M (2012) Computers and Creativity: the Road Ahead. In McCormack, J and d'Inverno, M (eds) *Computers and Creativity*. Berlin: Springer

Repenning, A, Webb, D and Ioannidou, A (2010) Scalable game design and the development of a checklist for getting computational thinking into public schools. In Proceedings of the 41st ACM Technical Symposium on Computer Science Education (SIGCSE '10), 265–269. New York: ACM Press.

Saavedra, AR and Opfer, VD (2012) Learning 21st-century skills requires 21st-century teaching. *Phi Delta Kappan*, 94(2), 8–13.

Settle, A, Franke, B, Hansen, R, Spaltro, F, Jurisson, C, Rennert-May, C and Wildeman, B (2012) Infusing computational thinking into the middle- and high-school curriculum. Proceedings of the 17th ACM annual conference on innovation and technology in computer science education, 3–5 July 2012, Haifa, Israel.

Tinari, FD and Khandke, K (2000) From rhythm and blues to Broadway: Using music to teach economics. *The Journal of Economic Education*, 31(3), 253–270.

Wing, JM (2008) Computational thinking and thinking about computing. *Philosophical Transactions of the Royal Society of London A: Mathematical, Physical and Engineering Sciences*, 366(1881), 3717–3725.

Chapter 3

ARTISTS

The process of preparing programs for a digital computer is especially attractive, not only because it can be economically and scientifically rewarding, but also because it can be an aesthetic experience much like composing poetry or music.

Knuth (1968)

Science is what we understand well enough to explain to a computer. Art is everything else we do.

Knuth (1996)

Introduction

This chapter will provide ways of linking art and computing activities together in the classroom by using practical art skills to explore ways of representing data and applying computational thinking to produce art.

Art and programming have been linked from the very beginning, both inspiring each other. The first programmable devices, some have argued, were musical automata, followed by weaving devices (Koetsier, 2001) such as the Jacquard Loom, which used punch cards to store and allow the replication of woven patterns. The punch cards went on to inspire Charles Babbage and later IBM used punch cards from the 1900s up to the early 1960s as their main means of data storage.

The idea of Pointillism, using small dots of colour to make up an image, is essentially how screens work on a computer – except we then call them picture elements or pixels. There is even Algorithmic Art and Generative Art (Pearson, 2011) where algorithms are used to create art.

The figure on p.52 was drawn using a simulation (Menegus, 2016) of a physical (and intricate) drawing device called a Cycloid Drawing Machine (Freedman, 2015).

Coming full circle, the Museum of Modern Art in New York has a section devoted to Computer Art including games (MoMA, 2012) as well as examples of using computers to make art. The subjects of computing and art continue to overlap. Google now is working on Project Jacquard (Google, 2016), which uses computers to weave

Figure 3.1   Algorithmic art

conductible threads into fabrics. These are then attached to tiny connectors and circuits so that we can interact with objects such as clothes or furniture.

Learning Outcomes

At the end of this chapter you should be able to:

- design and lead an unplugged activity that integrates practical art and computing;
- develop children's understanding of computing concepts such as sequences, selection and loops in the context of generative art;
- introduce children to binary representation and data representation through art and design.

Links to Teachers' Standards

The following Teachers' Standards are particularly relevant to this chapter:

TS1b Set goals that stretch and challenge pupils of all backgrounds, abilities and dispositions.
TS2d Demonstrate knowledge and understanding of how pupils learn and how this impacts on teaching.

TS3a Have a secure knowledge of the relevant subject(s) and curriculum areas, foster and maintain pupils' interest in the subject, and address misunderstandings.

TS4a Impart knowledge and develop understanding through effective use of lesson time.

TS4b Promote a love of learning and children's intellectual curiosity.

TS4e Contribute to the design and provision of an engaging curriculum within the relevant subject area(s).

TS5b Have a secure understanding of how a range of factors can inhibit pupils' ability to learn, and how best to overcome these.

(DfE, 2011)

Links to National Curriculum Programmes of Study

Art and design

Key Stage 1

Pupils should be taught:

- to develop a wide range of art and design techniques;
- about the work of a range of artists.

Key Stage 2

Pupils should be taught:

- to improve their mastery of art and design techniques;
- about great artists, architects and designers in history.

(DfE, 2013)

Unplugged Activity 1: Sol's solutions

Overview

Sol LeWitt (1928–2007) was an artist who did not always create his own artworks. Instead, he came up with an idea of what the artworks should look like and wrote instructions and diagrams to explain to other people how to create them.

In this activity we are going to focus on a certain type of LeWitt's art, which is made up of coloured or black-and-white stripes.

Children will create a set of instructions that they could give to another person to create the art. It is worth noting that LeWitt made some of his instructions deliberately ambiguous as his focus was on the artistic process, whereas in this activity, children will need to be exact and precise in order to meet the requirements of the computing curriculum.

Figure 3.2 *Spoleto* by Sol LeWitt

(Source: **https://commons.wikimedia.org**)

Computational thinking features developed

Writing a precise set of unambiguous instructions for another person to create a piece of art will require children to produce an *algorithm*. They will need to *debug* this algorithm by testing it in a draft version first and spotting any ambiguities, and then changing or correcting their algorithm.

Children will also need to break down the piece of artwork into its component parts to be able to produce the algorithm. This is an important skill within computational thinking called **decomposition,** which enables us to break large, complex problems down into smaller, manageable chunks. Using this terminology is not a specific requirement of the National Curriculum, but it is useful for children to develop the correct vocabulary so that they can discuss their learning. Decomposition can also be linked to the idea of working systematically to solve numeracy problems.

Cross-curricular links

Art and Design
Children will learn about Sol LeWitt's approach to creating art and will use art materials to create their finished piece.

Numeracy
Children will use rulers as measuring tools to accurately draw shapes and apply their knowledge of fractions to be able to divide the shapes into smaller blocks of colour.

Literacy
Children will use imperative verbs in their instructions.

Age range

Key Stage 1 and Key Stage 2.

lesson plan

Learning outcomes

'I can' statements:

- I can write a set of instructions to create a piece of art.
- I can improve my instructions.
- I can look at a piece of art and break it down into smaller parts.

Need to know

Algorithms are processes or sets of rules, which can be written as flowcharts, as written language, or as pseudocode. Pseudocode is an informal description using the structure of a programming language but written in a way that humans can understand. Well-written algorithms are:

- unambiguous, so there is no room for misinterpretation;

- precise, using exact language or diagrams to explain the steps;

- efficient, for example using a loop to repeat a pattern of commands rather than writing them out several times.

In this activity, drawing a square contains a repeating pattern of drawing a line and turning 90 degrees. Pupils will need to be precise in the way that they describe the lengths of the square and unambiguous about the need to put the writing tool on to the paper first.

Key words and questions

measure, divide, centimetres, colour, straight, right angle, square, length, half, quarter, horizontal, vertical, algorithm, debug

- How would a robot carry out that instruction?

- How can you make that instruction clearer for someone else to follow?

Resources

- A range of artworks by Sol LeWitt to use as a discussion starter.

- Art materials as required.

- Specific pieces of art in the style of Sol LeWitt to reproduce, for example:

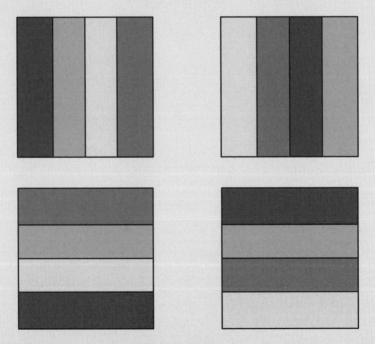

Figure 3.3 Art in the style of Sol LeWitt (minus colour)

Activities

Time	Activity	Resources
10 mins	Introduction • Introduce the art of Sol LeWitt, showing examples of his work. • Children discuss in small groups the question 'What are the key features of this type of art?' • Feedback as a whole class, drawing out vocabulary such as straight lines, curved lines, stripes of colour, squares, triangles. • Explain that Sol LeWitt has not created all these pictures himself. Instead he has written instructions to give to other people to create them. In this activity, we are going to work like Sol LeWitt and write instructions called algorithms to create art.	Examples of Sol LeWitt's art.
10 mins	Starter activity • Ask children to work in pairs and write simple instructions that someone else could follow to draw a 10 cm straight line. • Demonstrate that they will need to use 'bossy' verbs such as 'draw', 'put' and 'get' (imperatives). • Feedback as a whole class and draw on some of the answers to create model instructions, e.g. 1. Get a pencil, piece of paper and ruler 2. Draw a line with the pencil starting at 0 cm and finishing at 10 cm on the ruler • Discuss what will happen if the algorithms are not precise enough and draw out the need to debug the instructions to make them clearer.	Pencils and paper or whiteboards and whiteboard pens. Make rulers available if children need these to try out their algorithms.
15 mins	Writing the instructions • Give each child a small piece of art based on Sol LeWitt's designs. • Ask children to create a set of written instructions that they could give to another person to create this piece of art.	Pencils and paper or whiteboards and whiteboard pens. Individual small pieces of art, one per child (see notes on differentiation).
20 mins	Testing the instructions • Pair the children in mixed-ability pairs so that they can test their instructions. At this stage, the stripes of colour can be lightly shaded with coloured pencils. • Encourage the children to refine their instructions to make them more precise, possibly by writing the changes in a different coloured pencil.	Pencils and paper, ruler, coloured paper.
5 mins	Plenary • Choose some examples of instructions of algorithms which have been debugged and highlight these to the whole class. • Discuss what kinds of changes made the algorithms more precise.	Examples of children's work.

Scope for differentiation and extension

This activity can be simplified by using only black-and-white pieces of art with less stripes or made more challenging by using pieces of art with more complex patterns.

Figure 3.4 Examples of simple pieces of art

Younger children could write instructions to potato print or paint stripes of colour inside a pre-printed square.

The samples of artwork could include repeating patterns of stripes rather than random stripes to develop the idea of using repetition in algorithms.

This activity could be extended to go on and create an art gallery of pieces in the style of LeWitt which could then be used for a classroom display or a virtual display on the school website.

In order to do this, children will need to work in pairs with the following roles:

- One child will take the role of the artist and read out their instructions.

- The other child will take the role of the creator who carries out the instructions and creates the piece of art. They will need to carry out the instructions exactly as they are read out.

- The children could then swap roles and repeat the activity.

You might relate this to the process of *pair programming*, in which two programmers work together as a driver and a navigator, with one writing the code while the other reviews each line.

It is important to select art materials that can quickly create blocks of colour for this activity. It would work well in an outdoor space, for example by painting on large sheets of paper taped to the floor or using chalks on tarmac. The artwork could also be produced on a smaller scale in the classroom, using paints, chalks or prints on paper.

Unplugged Activity 2: Rocketing numbers and images

Overview

This activity explores image representation by making giant images pixel by pixel and using binary numbers. It can be linked to the concept of Pointillism in art, which uses small dots of colour to make up an image. Computer screens essentially use the same technique.

Children start with a copy of the grid below. They use a light colour such as yellow to fill in squares to draw a rocket. After that, they put a 1 in the coloured blocks instead of a 0.

Children produce additional diagrams showing the stages of the rocket taking off in order to animate the sequence.

If you are working with Key Stage 2 children you could now explore another way of representing their image using binary numbers.

For each row children add the columns together that have a 1 in them; so for row 3 (third row from the top, the columns with 1s in are 16, 8 and 4 with the total of 28).

128	64	32	16	8	4	2	1
0	0	0	0	0	0	0	0
0	0	0	0	0	0	0	0
0	0	0	0	0	0	0	0
0	0	0	0	0	0	0	0
0	0	0	0	0	0	0	0
0	0	0	0	0	0	0	0
0	0	0	0	0	0	0	0
0	0	0	0	0	0	0	0
0	0	0	0	0	0	0	0
0	0	0	0	0	0	0	0
0	0	0	0	0	0	0	0
0	0	0	0	0	0	0	0
0	0	0	0	0	0	0	0
0	0	0	0	0	0	0	0
0	0	0	0	0	0	0	0
0	0	0	0	0	0	0	0

Figure 3.5 Grid 1

128	64	32	16	8	4	2	1
0	0	0	0	1	0	0	0
0	0	0	0	1	0	0	0
0	0	0	1	1	1	0	0
0	0	0	1	1	1	0	0
0	0	0	1	1	1	0	0
0	0	0	1	1	1	0	0
0	0	0	1	1	1	0	0
0	0	0	1	1	1	0	0
0	0	0	1	1	1	0	0
0	0	0	1	1	1	0	0
0	0	0	1	1	1	0	0
0	0	1	1	1	1	1	0
0	0	1	1	1	1	1	0
0	1	1	0	0	0	1	1
0	1	0	0	0	0	0	1

Figure 3.6 Grid 2

128	64	32	16	8	4	2	1
0	0	0	1	1	1	0	0
0	0	0	1	1	1	0	0
0	0	0	1	1	1	0	0
0	0	0	1	1	1	0	0
0	0	0	1	1	1	0	0
0	0	0	1	1	1	0	0
0	0	0	1	1	1	0	0
0	0	0	1	1	1	0	0
0	0	0	1	1	1	0	0
0	0	0	1	1	1	0	0
0	0	1	1	1	1	1	0
0	0	1	1	1	1	1	0
0	1	1	0	0	0	1	1
0	1	0	0	0	0	0	1
0	0	0	0	0	0	0	0
0	0	0	0	0	0	0	0

Grid 3

128	64	32	16	8	4	2	1
0	0	1	1	1	1	1	0
0	0	1	1	1	1	1	0
0	1	1	0	0	0	1	1
0	1	0	0	0	0	0	1
0	0	0	0	0	0	0	0
0	0	0	0	0	0	0	0
0	0	0	0	0	0	0	0
0	0	0	0	0	0	0	0
0	0	0	0	0	0	0	0
0	0	0	0	0	0	0	0
0	0	0	0	0	0	0	0
0	0	0	0	0	0	0	0
0	0	0	0	0	0	0	0
0	0	0	0	0	0	0	0
0	0	0	0	0	0	0	0
0	0	0	0	0	0	0	0

Grid 4

Figure 3.7 Grids 3 and 4 showing the rocket taking off

Table 3.1 Example table

Row	Columns used	Total
1	8	8
2	8	8
3	16+8+4	28
4	16+8+4	28
5	16+8+4	28
6	16+8+4	28
7	16+8+4	28
8	16+8+4	28
9	16+8+4	28
10	16+8+4	28
11	16+8+4	28
12	16+8+4	28
13	32+16+8+4+2	62
14	32+16+8+4+2	62
15	64+32+2+1	99
16	64+1	65

The next stage is to convert each row into a single number. In each row, children find the cells that have a 1 in them. They write down the numbers at the tops of these columns. For instance, the third row has three 1s, so we should write down the numbers 16, 8, and 4. We now add up these numbers to find the single number that represents the row ($16 + 8 + 4 = 28$ in this example).

This shows that an image can be turned into a set of numbers. The numbers in 1s and 0s in Figure 3.6 are the binary numbers of those on the same rows in Table 3.1.

As an additional activity, children can film a short animated sequence to show their rocket taking off.

Computational thinking features developed

Using an *algorithm* to turn an image into a set of numbers. An algorithm is a precise sequence of activities, describing how to solve a problem.

This is essentially about *data representation*, showing in two ways how an object can be represented by a set of numbers. The second part of this is demonstrating that the numbers in Figure 3.6 for the 'rocket' are actually binary.

Abstraction: we can model the image as a set of numbers.

Sequence is a set of activities with each following on from another in the same order.

Cross-curricular links

Numeracy

Children will use addition to turn an image into a set of numbers. As an extension, the idea of binary number equivalents can be explored by adding zeros to the grid in Figure 3.6.

Age range

Key Stages 1 and 2.

Lesson plan

Learning outcomes

'I can' statements:

- I can use numbers to represent something different.
- I can follow an algorithm to represent an image as a set of numbers.
- I can use binary representation.

Need to know

Binary is how we can think of information being stored in a machine, as 1s and 0s. Each 0 or 1 is a bit (short for **B**inary dig**it**). A bit is the smallest unit of data in a computer. It is often easier to represent these numbers as blocks of 8 bits or a *byte*, as a single number. A *byte* is the unit most computers use to represent a character such as a letter or a number. Computer memory is described in terms of kilobytes (1,024 *bytes*), megabytes (1,048,576 *bytes*), gigabytes (1,073,741,824 *bytes*) and terabytes (approximately a trillion bytes).

Pixel means Picture Element.

Key words and questions

add, binary, data, representation, sequence, algorithm

- What do you know about how computers represent images?

- How do computers store information?

- What would other images look like as numbers?

Resources

- The blank grid.

- Art materials as required.

- Optional: device with a digital camera and software.

Activities (Key Stage 1)

Time	Activity	Resources
10 mins	Introduction • Explore what children already know about data representation. • Explain the idea of using a grid to make an image. • The tasks are to explore ways of representing images through numbers and to make a rocket appear to take off.	Blank grid on screen Filled-in grid on screen
20 mins	Starter activity • Working in threes, ask the children to fill in the blank grid to match the match the 'rocket' grid. Each child has a different grid to colour (either grid 2, 3 or 4).	Pencils and blank grids or whiteboards and whiteboard pens Make coloured pencils available
15 mins	First animation • The children between themselves decide on the order of the grids. • Write a 'shooting script' showing the order of the grids. • If a digital device is available: • Photograph each filled-in grid; • Put them together to animate the rocket take-off based on the shooting script. • If digital device not available: • Grids are put them together to make the rocket; take-off based on the shooting script.	A device with a digital camera Software or app to combine the images into an animation
15 mins	Second animation • Improve the shooting scripts and grids to enhance the animation. Example ideas: • Add flames to the grids. • Include a blank grid to show the rocket has left the page. • Add a further grid so that the movement is smoother between grids 3 and 4.	A device with a digital camera Software or app to combine the images into an animation
20 mins	Plenary • Highlight that the shooting script is an algorithm and shows a sequence of instructions. • How could the animation be improved or debugged?	

Activities (Key Stage 2)

Time	Activity	Resources
5 mins	Introduction • Explain the idea of using a grid to make an image.	Blank grid on screen. Filled-in grid on screen.
20 mins	Starter activity • Working in pairs, ask the children to fill in the grid to match the 'rocket' grid.	Pencils and blank grids or whiteboards and whiteboard pens. Make coloured pencils available.
25 mins	Writing the instructions • Go through the first two rows of the filled grid explaining the idea of adding columns to give a number. • Ask children work through the rest.	Pencils and paper or whiteboards and whiteboard pens.
30 mins	Plenary • Discuss the idea of 0 or 1 states equating to on or off. • Relate this to the binary numeral system.	Whiteboard.

Scope for differentiation and extension

Try the activity with another picture such as a simple face.

Can you turn these numbers into a picture using the table in Figure 3.5?

255, 129, 129, 129, 129, 129, 129, 255?

Unplugged Activity 3: Thomas's tangles

Overview

In this activity children will explore abstract patterns using randomness within an algorithm.

Using crayons, pencils or pens, children will follow an algorithm to create a random drawing. This could be done in pairs using squared paper.

Person A: Rolls the dice and reads out the instructions.

Person B: Is the robot carrying out the instructions.

When the starting or central square is blocked and a new central square is needed, the roles of A and B swap (so A is the 'robot' and B rolls the dice and reads out the instruction). The roles keep swapping.

Here is the algorithm:

```
Start from a random square - call it the centre square
Repeat until end of game
```

```
If die roll = 1

     Roll die for number of moves

     Check for blocks

     If not blocked then

          move die roll number of steps up the
          page

If die roll = 2

     Roll die for number of moves

     Check for blocks

     If not blocked then

          move die roll number of steps down the
          page

If die roll = 3

     Roll die for number of moves

     Check for blocks

     If not blocked then

          move die roll number of steps to the
          left

If die roll = 4

     Roll die for number of moves

     Check for blocks

     If not blocked then

          move die roll number of steps to the
          right

If die roll = 5

     Roll die

     If die = 1 change colour to Red

     If die = 2 change colour to Blue

     If die = 3 change colour to Black

     If die = 4 change colour to Red
```

```
            If die = 5 change colour to Orange

            If die = 6 change colour to Yellow

            If die roll = 6

                 Return to current centre square

Check for blocks:

     If pathway blocked do not move then

          reroll die

     If number of spaces in the direction > die roll
     then

          move until blocked

     If all pathways blocked then

          choose a new centre square
```

Computational thinking features developed

Using an *algorithm* to produce a randomised picture.

Refining the algorithm.

Identifying computing constructs such as *sequences*, *selection* and *loops*.

Cross-curricular links

Art and Design
Children will learn about generative art by using art materials to create the finished piece based on an algorithm. They could go on to explore examples of generative art in Scratch.

Age range

Key Stage 2.

Lesson plan

Learning outcomes

'I can' statements

- I can produce a picture by following an algorithm.
- I can follow an algorithm that uses randomness.
- I can 'debug' or refine an algorithm with my own ideas.
- I can identify computing constructs such as *sequences*, *selection* and *loops* within an algorithm.

Need to know

Algorithms are sequences of instructions that can have randomness built into them. They may select from *conditional statements* such as an 'if-then' statement which may perform different actions depending on whether a Boolean condition is true or false. Algorithms may include loops such as 'repeat until'.

Key words and questions

random, abstract, selection, sequence, loop, conditional statement

- What changes would you make to the algorithm?

- Can you find an example of a conditional statement in the algorithm?

- Can you find an example of a loop in the algorithm?

Resources

- The algorithm copied for each pair of pupils.

- One die per pair. They could make their own dice.

- Squared paper and coloured pencils.

Activities

Time	Activity	Resources
15 mins	Introduction • Explain that the idea of randomness is going to be used to produce a picture. • Go through the algorithm using the terms selection, sequence, loop and conditional statement.	A copy of finished picture. A copy of the algorithm per group.
40 mins	Starter activity • Working in pairs, ask the children to take turns with the two roles. • Person A: Rolls the dice and reads out the instructions – using the algorithm. • Person B: Is the 'robot' carrying out the instructions. • When the starting or central square is blocked and a new central square is needed the roles of A and B swap (so A is the 'robot' and B rolls the dice and reads out the instruction). • The roles keep swapping.	A copy of the algorithm. At least one die per group. Squared paper and six different coloured pencils.
30 mins	Plenary • Show examples of the children's work. • What changes would they make to the algorithm?	Show examples of children's work.

Scope for differentiation and extension

For a follow-on 'plugged' activity you could aim to build part of this in Scratch. As a suggestion, build it so that only a single 'spiral' of one colour is used.

Examples of coding and art projects in Scratch can be found here:

https://uk.pinterest.com/helencaldwel/coding-art/

Discussion

Teaching the Computing curriculum can seem daunting at first and you may find that some pupils seem to have a greater understanding of the subject than the teacher. However, when compared with art, the same could also be said to apply; many teachers deliver successful art lessons without being able to draw or paint. In these classroom situations, the teacher's role is that of the facilitator who creates the right conditions for pupils to learn (Papert, 1993) rather than an expert who has all the skills and answers.

The introduction of the Computing curriculum aims to change children from consumers into creators of technology. This idea aligns with widespread good practice in teaching, where pupils learn best by immersively doing activities rather than passively receiving information.

In the first decade of the twenty-first century, Jeanette Wing wrote an article encouraging computing professionals and educators to recognise computational thinking as an essential skill for everyone (Wing, 2006). At this stage, there was no encompassing definition of what this skill involved and other educators argued for the need for a range of computing skills including *computational doing* (Denning, 2009).

Further research has begun to shape the meaning of computational thinking. One definition is that it is a set of thought processes used by a human to be able to frame a problem and devise a solution to it in a form that can be carried out by a computer (Wing, 2011; Barr *et al.*, 2011).

In the USA, work to embed computational thinking in the curriculum has focused on a set of nine different skills (Barr and Stephenson, 2011). In the UK, computational thinking has been positioned at the heart of the new Computing curriculum (DfE, 2013) and the most widely accepted implementation is a set of five techniques:

1. Abstraction – removing unnecessary complexity and detail from a problem.

2. Decomposition – breaking down a problem into smaller component parts.

3. Generalisation – spotting patterns in problems that can be re-applied and adapted to use in other problems.

4. Algorithmic thinking – defining a solution as a logical step-by-step process.

5. Evaluation – assessing a solution to make sure it is effective, efficient and fit for purpose.

(Selby and Woollard, 2013)

Solving real-world problems is at the core of computational thinking. Wing referred to this (Wing, 2011) in examples such as using a series of pipelining techniques where the output of one element determines the next input to devise the most efficient way of presenting diplomas or serving lunch at a cafeteria. One way of demonstrating progression in computational thinking is to have students create algorithms for descriptive, closed problems to start with (for example, how to make a sandwich or clean your teeth) and then move on to open-ended problems to find the best solution (for example, what is the fastest way that we can collect all the class work up and hand it into the teacher for marking?).

The very nature of the cross-curricular learning opportunities in the primary phase means that it can be challenging to separate the learning in computing from that of the other subjects. Some successful strategies for assessment include the following:

- Self-assessment: when debugging algorithms, children are evaluating their work and improving on previous versions. It can be useful to keep copies of the 'wrong' algorithms as well as the final versions in order to evidence this.

- Peer-assessment: working in pairs is a good habit to establish in these activities. One pupil can create an algorithm, and their partner can test it and feedback their findings constructively. Peer feedback can be evidenced in different ways, for example by comments in a different colour pencil or by commenting online on a class blog.

- Open questioning: asking questions such as: How does this algorithm work? What will happen if a robot follows these instructions exactly as they are written? Why will this algorithm complete the task successfully?

(Computing at School, 2013)

Summary and Key Points

Although art and computing may seem an unlikely combination to teach in the primary curriculum, this chapter has given exemplar activities which can integrate the two subjects successfully.

By writing an algorithm to create a piece of artwork, learners will practise creating precise step-by-step instructions, testing these with a partner and debugging any errors.

Thinking about how images are represented digitally on a computer screen strengthens learners' understanding of the world around them and introduces the concept of data representation.

Due to the relatively recent addition of Computing to the National Curriculum, there is ongoing debate and research into effective pedagogy for the subject. However, a firm foundation has already been laid by the work of organisations such as Computing at School, and the cross-curricular approach outlined here can assist in ensuring coverage of the Programme of Study to meet the curriculum requirements.

Further reading

Liukas, L (2015) Activity 7 The Robots. In *Hello Ruby – Adventures in Coding*. New York: Feiwel and Friends, 94–97.

Schofield, S (2016) Generative Artworks. Available from: **www.simonschofield.net**

Turner, S (2016) 3 'Art' Scratch Projects. Available from: **http://compuationalthinking.blogspot. co.uk/2016/03/3-of-my-scratch-projects-for-week.html** accessed on: 12/3/2016.

References

Barr, D, Harrion, J and Conery, L (2011) *Computational Thinking: A Digital Age Skill for Everyone.* Leading and Learning with Technology, ISTE, March/April 2011. Available from **www.csta.acm.org/ Curriculum/sub/CurrFiles/LLCTArticle.pdf** (accessed 26 December 2015).

Barr, V and Stephenson, C (2011) Bringing computational thinking to K-12. *ACM Inroads*, 2 (1), 48–54. Available from **http://csta.acm.org/Curriculum/sub/CurrFiles/BarrStephensonInroadsArticle.pdf** (accessed 26 December 2015).

Computing at School (2013) *Computing in the National Curriculum: A guide for primary teachers*. Available from **www.computingatschool.org.uk/data/uploads/CASPrimaryComputing.pdf** (accessed 13 March 2016).

Denning, Peter J (2009) Beyond computational thinking. *Communications of the ACM*, 52 (6), 28–30. Available from **http://sgd.cs.colorado.edu/wiki/images/7/71/Denning.pdf** (accessed 26 December 2015).

Department for Education (DfE) (2011) *Teachers' Standards*. Available from **www.gov.uk/government/ uploads/system/uploads/attachment_data/file/283566/Teachers_standard_information.pdf** (accessed 23 December 2015).

Department for Education (DfE) (2013) *National Curriculum in England: Computing programmes of study*. London: Department for Education.

Freedman, J (2015) Cycloid Drawing Machine. Available from **www.kickstarter.com/ projects/1765367532/cycloid-drawing-machine** (accessed 3 March 2016).

Google (2016) Project Jacquard. Available from **https://www.google.com/atap/project-jacquard/** (accessed 1 March 2016).

Knuth, D (1968) Preface, *The Art of Programming*, volume 1. Boston, MA: Addison-Wesley.

Knuth, D (1996) Foreword. In Petkovsek, M, Wilf, H and, Zeilberger, D, *A=B*. Natick, MA: A K Peters/ CRC Press, vii.

Koetsier, T (2001) On the prehistory of programmable machines: Musical automata, looms, calculators. *Mechanism and Machine Theory*, 36(5), 589–603.

Menegus, B (2016) CDMS: Built with processing. Available from **http://wheelof.com/sketch/** (accessed 4 March 2016).

MoMA (2012) *MoMA| Video Games.* Available from **www.moma.org/explore/inside_out/2012/11/29/ video-games-14-in-the-collection-for-starters/** (accessed 1 March 2016).

National Curriculum in England: *Art and design programmes of study – key stages 1 and 2*, Department for Education (11 September 2013).

Papert, S (1993) *The Children's Machine: Rethinking schools in the age of the computer.* New York: Basic Books.

Pearson, M (2011) *Generative Art: A practical guide using Processing.* New York: Manning, 3–12.

Selby, C and Woollard, J (2013) *Computational Thinking: The developing definition*. University of Southampton. Available from **http://eprints.soton.ac.uk/356481/7/Selby_Woollard_bg_soton_ eprints.pdf** (accessed 26 December 2015).

The Art Story (2016) *Sol LeWitt.* Available from **www.theartstory.org/artist-lewitt-sol.htm** (accessed on 6 March 2016).

Wing, J (2006) Computational thinking. *Communications of the ACM,* 49, 33 –35.Available from **www.cs.cmu.edu/~15110-s13/Wing06-ct.pdf** (accessed 26 December 2015).

Wing, J (2011) Computational thinking – What and why. *The Link – News from the School of Computer Science,* Issue 6.0, Spring 2011. Available from **www.cs.cmu.edu/sites/default/files/11-399_The_Link_ Newsletter-3.pdf** (accessed on 26 December 2015).

Chapter 4

EXPLORERS

The Internet is the world's largest library. It's just that all the books are on the floor.

John Allen Paulos

Introduction

'Unplugged' means more than using pencil and paper instead of a computer. There are many ways of learning and ways to make learning engaging. This chapter is about using kinaesthetic activities to illustrate computational ideas. In these activities, children will use their bodies to explore algorithms, abstraction and logical thinking, and how computers themselves can persevere and collaborate to solve complex tasks.

We do this through three activities and their outline lesson plans:

- *Sorting networks* show how algorithms work and can be designed, through the children role-playing data as it is manipulated and passed through a data-processing algorithm.

- *Plugging in* shows how abstraction is used in computer networks to hide some messy low-level details from the high-level idea of just communicating.

- *Riding the internet* gets children to role-play data packets as they move around the internet in response to website requests.

Learning Outcomes

At the end of this chapter you should be able to:

- show how some algorithms can be demonstrated by children representing the data that flows as the algorithm is executed;
- demonstrate how details can be hidden by abstraction;
- illustrate some simple ideas of how computers can persevere and collaborate.

Links to Teachers' Standards

The following Teachers' Standards are particularly relevant to this chapter:

TS1 Set high expectations which inspire, motivate and challenge pupils.
TS3 Demonstrate good subject and curriculum knowledge.
TS4 Plan and teach well structured lessons.

(DfE, 2011)

Unplugged Activity 1: Sorting networks

Overview

Sorting is often used to explain algorithms, as it's a simple problem for people to understand, it's easy to see if the algorithm works, and there are many different algorithms that get to the same result in various ways. In this activity, your children will represent an algorithm as a pattern drawn in chalk on a playground and they will become the data the algorithm operates on.

A sorting network is a way of representing how an unsorted series of things can be ordered. (The things being sorted can be anything, so long as we can define an order on them. We could sort numbers, letters, schools in a league table, or anything else we can meaningfully compare. We'll use numbers in these examples.) The network is a group of wires, one for each thing being sorted, that run from left to right. Comparators run up and down between two wires; when there's an object at both ends of the comparator, they're swapped if they're out of order, but remain in place if they're in order.

Figure 4.1a shows a sorting network for four items; Figure 4.1b shows how it sorts a set of numbers. Try it with different numbers as input: it always works.

In this activity, you will draw out sorting networks on the playground, using chalk or whatever comes to hand. When you draw the network, first draw all the wires and

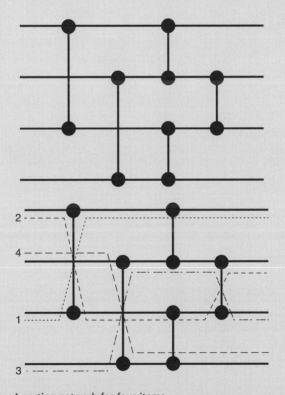

Figures 4.1a and 4.1b   A sorting network for four items

mark one side of the network to be the 'small' side. This is the top in the diagrams here, and each comparison should end with the small number at this side.

Children will each take a piece of card with a number on it. They'll start at the beginning of the wires and run along them until they reach a node.

At each node, the child will wait until someone arrives at the opposite end of the comparator. If necessary, they'll swap, so the child with the smallest number is at the top. Both children then move along their wire until the next node. When all the children have reached the end, their numbers should be in order.

Repeat the activity with the next set of children. The numbers given out need not be consecutive or start at one, so long as the children can check whether the numbers are sorted or not.

Computational thinking features developed

Algorithmic thinking, by following a simple procedure. Each comparison operation is very simple, but the combination of them does something quite complex.

Logical thinking, to predict what will happen when different arrangements of numbers are fed into the sorting network and how different sorting networks will behave when built up from simpler ones.

Abstraction, to extend a network to more inputs.

Cross-curricular links

Numeracy
The idea of sorting and comparing objects.

Age range

Key Stage 1: using sorting networks.

Key Stage 2: comparing different sorting networks for the same number of inputs, creating new sorting networks.

Lesson plan

Learning outcomes

After this activity, students should be able to do and achieve these:

- I can use a sorting network to sort people.
- I can describe how repeated comparisons and swaps, in the right order, can sort a group of objects.
- I can generalise a sorting network.

Key words and questions

Sorting – putting a group of things in order.

Comparable – two things are comparable if we can say one is smaller, earlier, or comes before another. If we can't decide how to compare objects, we can't define how to sort them.

Swapping – a basis for a lot of different ways of sorting. Two objects are compared and swapped if they're out of order. Which objects are compared when defines the sorting algorithm.

If all we can do is compare two items and swap them, can we sort many things in order?

How many comparisons and swaps do we need to do? How does this change as we change the number of items to be sorted?

Are there different ways of sorting items, which all work, but have different numbers of comparisons?

Activities

Time	Teacher activity	Student activity	Resources
10 mins	Before the lesson, teacher draws out a simple sorting network, perhaps the network for 8 items in Figure 4.2. Make sure to mark the stopping points for use of comparators.	Students might be able to do this, but teachers should carefully check the network is correct. Even a small mistake can make nothing work!	Chalk, string, etc. to mark the network. Perhaps small cones to mark the ends of comparators.
5 mins	Teacher explains the idea of sorting networks, shows some examples on a handout or screen.		
5 mins	Teacher takes children outside, explains rules of how to use the drawn-out sorting network. Stress that children must wait at a comparator until someone arrives at the other end!		
10 mins		Groups of children take cards, run through the sorting network, check that it works.	Cards with numbers.
10 mins	Teacher extends the network to include one more wire.	Children run through the expanded network.	
10 mins	Teacher sums up the activity, pointing out the nature of sorting and how different networks can yield the same result.		

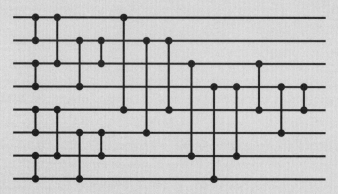

Figure 4.2   A sorting network for eight items

Variations, differentiation and extensions

You can draw the networks on to paper and distribute them as worksheets. Children can try different arrangements as inputs and check the network always sorts them, drawing the paths of different objects using different colours.

You could get students to sort other things, such as letters of the alphabet or even names (if you want to stress alphabetical ordering). If the sorting goes wrong, you can ask children to backtrack to detect and fix errors: at some point, a pair will come out of a comparison in the wrong order.

Some children may struggle with the idea that numbers can be in sorted order, even if the numbers aren't sequential.

Key Stage 2 children could be asked to design their own sorting networks for different numbers of inputs. The trick is to build them up simply. One-wire and two-wire sorting networks are trivial (Figure 4.3). A three-wire network can be built from a two-wire network by adding a new wire at the bottom. We can 'sink' the largest value to this wire by adding two comparators, then sorting the remaining values using the existing two-wire network (Figure 4.4). A four-wire network can be built from a three-wire network in the same way (Figure 4.5). You can continue to build up networks in this way for any size, but there are other ways to build sorting networks that have fewer comparators. (The four-wire network in Figure 4.5 has six comparators, while the four-wire network in Figure 4.1 only needs five.)

An extension activity could be to ask these children to come up with other sorting networks that are still correct, but which have fewer networks. The *Wikipedia* article on sorting networks lists the minimum of comparators for different numbers of wires.

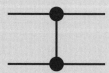

Figure 4.3   A two-wire sorting network

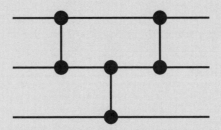

Figure 4.4   A three-wire sorting network, showing the inclusion of a two-wire sorting network

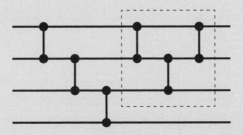

Figure 4.5   A four-wire sorting network, showing the inclusion of a three-wire sorting network

Success criteria and assessment

Children will have met the learning criteria if they can explain the notion of sorting and can identify when a group of numbers (or letters or names) is sorted correctly. Key Stage 2 children should be able to show how a sorting can be enlarged, given one that already works.

Unplugged Activity 2: Riding the internet

Overview

In this activity, children develop their understanding of how the Internet works by looking at how messages are split into packets, and how different physical connection types affect how messages are transported. The children will play 'the packets game' which illustrates the function of these systems by sending packets of information around the room to their destination. This progresses to packets of information being sent via different communication methods, to show how different types of connection vary by bandwidth and reliability.

Parts of this activity have been inspired by Phil Bagge's work on 'Network, Internet & Web Search Planning' (**http://code-it.co.uk/**) and by a Code.org activity, 'The Internet'.

Computational thinking features developed

This activity requires pupils to *generalise* what they already know about the Internet in order to build on their previous knowledge of methods of *data transmission* and *data representation*. It also requires them to use *abstraction* to see how entire messages can be passed even if only parts of the message are moving at one time.

Cross-curricular links

Literacy
Years 5 and 6 Key Stage 2:

Identify the audience for and purpose of the writing, select the appropriate form and use other similar writing as models for their own.

Use further organisational and presentational devices to structure text and to guide the reader.

Age range

This activity has been planned for Key Stage 2 children who already have background knowledge of computer networks and some understanding of how the Internet works.

Lesson plan

Learning objectives

Computational thinking

- To generalise what children know about how the internet works.
- To explain data transmission using packets.

Computing

- To understand computer networks, including the internet.

Need to know

When information is moved across the internet, it is broken down into *packets*. Each packet contains a fragment of the information, along with data about the recipient of the information, how many packets make up the whole message, and so on. This is so that a single communication link between computers can be used for many different conversations at the same time, by interleaving the packets of different conversations. Also, packets can travel across the network by different routes to avoid *network congestion*.

Packets contain labels giving their source and destination, which message they're part of, which part of the message they are, and a *time to live* (TTL). The time to live is needed so that packets will eventually be discarded if there is no route available to the destination.

An analogy for packet switching is moving a lot of cargo from place to place by putting it in a variety of lorries. Each lorry can make its own route to the destination and the entire consignment can be reassembled when all the lorries have arrived. The alternative is for roads to be blocked to allow a single, very large lorry to go through, which causes problems for all the other road users.

Key words and questions

Packets – a small part of your data which is sent across a network.

- How does the packet know where to go?
- Why does the web page need to be broken into packets?

Activities

Packet game rules

A network is laid out on a playground or similar space. There are a number of router nodes inside the network, each with a pot or other container. The nodes on the edge are user nodes; each user node has a clearly visible label, such as a piece of paper taped to the back of a chair.

The children split into two groups. Each user node has a user at that chair; each user has a list of messages they need to send to other users. Each router node has a child representing the transmission capacity of that router. If there are more children than routers, have more than one child on a router; if there are fewer children, some routers will not have a child, but each router should be next to at least one occupied router.

The routers move packets around as they find them. They only move from their home router to an adjacent one, and back again. Starting at their router they pick a random packet card from their pot and mark off one 'time to live' tag. If the packet has run out of time to live, it goes in the bin. If the packet is still alive, the router sees where it should travel to and picks another router on the way. They then run to that router and drop the packet into the pot. If the pot has other packets waiting, the child will pick one of them. If the player's home router is on a sensible route for this packet, the child will mark off a 'time to live' tag and take it back of their home router.

If there is no packet that's sensible to collect, the child returns to their home router. If there are no packets at their home router, the child will run to a random adjacent router and look for packets.

Only one child can be putting packets into and out of the pot at a time. Other children at the node will have to wait their turn.

To send a message, the user writes down the message on as many packet cards as it needs. All packets start with a time to live of one or two steps longer than the longest route across the network (6 for the example in Figure 4.6). The user then attracts the attention of one of the routers. The router collects just one packet, returns to their home router, and carries on.

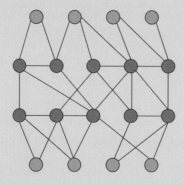

Figure 4.6 A sample communication network. Note that some 'obvious' connections are missing.

Eventually, the packets will move across the network from source to destination. If a packet arrives at the wrong user, it is discarded. When all the packets of a message arrive (in whatever order), the message has been successfully delivered.

Activities

Time	Teacher activity	Student activity	Resources
Before the lesson	Draw out a network on the playground, using chalk, ropes, or similar. Put a bucket or basket at each junction. Place chairs at the terminal nodes of the network, with a piece of paper attached to show the address.		
5 mins	Ask children to explain how the Internet works	Draw a quick diagram and explain to their partners.	Display key words such as router, server, ISP, underwater cables, etc.
10 mins	Explain that when a website is retrieved from the web server it is too big to travel in one chunk, so it's broken up into small pieces. Children are going to model this by playing 'the packets game'.		
5 mins	Model completing the packet information sheet (see Figure 4.7). Children can write a message to anyone in the room that is up to 3 packets long.	Children complete their message (or a couple of messages if there's time) on the packets sheet.	A copy of the packets sheet such as in Figure 4.7. Dice
10 mins	Explain the rules of the packet game. Model the start of a journey of a packet with one or two packets using just one user and two routers.		
	After a few minutes, either remove a connection between two router nodes, or slow down router children moving packets into or out of a router node's pot. After a while, children should notice the change and modify their routing decisions.	Play the packets game.	
	Spend some time reflecting on what the game was showing the children about the Internet.	Children explain what they have learned from the game.	

Success criteria and assessment

If pupils have met the learning outcomes, they will:

- be able to explain the term 'packet' and suggest the information that needs to be included on a packet;

- be able to explain how information can be split across packets and reconstructed by the recipient;

- understand that different packets in the same message can take different routes;

- appreciate that packets can become lost and explain what happens when this occurs.

Questioning will be particularly important in this exercise as there is no written recording. You can regularly make parallels with the real world such as when their internet is being slow or if there is a connection error. Keep swapping roles to check that children understand the role played by each part of the internet.

Scope for differentiation and extension

Support
You could support learners by introducing and reinforcing the concepts. Where learners may be overwhelmed, focus on just one thing at a time. It might be that they are just beginning to understand that a website is saved on a computer somewhere called a web server. Start here and then build upon their developing understanding in small chunks by slowly adding more complexity into the game.

Stretch
Encourage more confident children to think about everyone using the Internet at the same time and the distance that the data is having to travel. An outdoor lesson

To	**Bob**					
From	**Teacher**			(your name)		
Message		H	E	L	L	O
			B	O	B	
I		H	O	P	E		Y
O	U		A	R	E		L
Message Split 1/1, ①/②, 2/2, 1/3, 2/3, 3/3						
Time to live			6			

To	**Bob**					
From	**Teacher**			(your name)		
Message		E	A	R	N	I
		N	G		L	O
T	S					
Message Split 1/1, 1/2, ②/②, 1/3, 2/3, 3/3						
Time to live			7			

Figure 4.7 A teacher sends two packets of information to a student named Bob

---

The Client

The computer passes a request to the Internet that the user would like to look at a website, e.g. the user has used a web browser and typed in a URL such as www.bbc.co.uk

1. *Pass the website request to the Internet to retrieve the website.*
2. *When the website returns and is assembled in once piece, smile, click on something else and the whole process will start again!*

Figure 4.8   An example role card reminding children what they need to do. These are particularly useful if you keep swapping them around.

will reinforce the concept of information journeys. Children might also think about security issues such as what happens if a packet is intercepted.

Unplugged Activity 3: Getting 'plugged in'

Overview

In this activity, children build upon their basic understanding of how a computer network works by role-playing how different connections work. Some children will ask questions from lists they are given; others will be websites that have answers to those questions. The remaining children will be the network, moving questions and answers around, but with different reliability to represent different types of connection.

In line with the explorers theme, this activity is best undertaken on a large scale outdoors, emphasising the idea of information journeys.

Computational thinking features developed

This activity requires pupils to use *abstraction* to relate the physical activity to computer networks, relating the different ways of moving information physically to different types of network connection. As with Activity 2, the students can use *abstraction* to see that different communication methods can end up with the same result of a message moved from place to place.

Cross-curricular links

The activity uses questions and answers, which could be from any topic.

Age range

This activity is suitable for children in upper Key Stage 1 or Key Stage 2.

Lesson plan

Learning objectives

Computational thinking

- To explain an abstracted version of the Internet.
- To understand data transmission and representation in relation to the Internet.

Computing

- To explain how websites are retrieved from the Internet.
- To understand computer networks including the Internet and how they can provide services such as the World Wide Web.

Need to know

Computers communicate using a variety of physical systems, with different properties. For the purposes of this exercise, we can split them into three types: wired network connections, wireless connections (WiFi), and mobile phone connections. Wired connections are the fastest and most reliable. WiFi is not as fast and can be unreliable, especially when the computer is far from the access point, but has the advantage of being able to move around. Mobile connections are the most flexible, but are the slowest and least reliable.

Key words and questions

Network – what computers use to communicate with each other.

Reliability – how often things don't go wrong. This can be expressed as time between failures.

How does reliability affect speed data speed?

Which network type is best for different situations?

Activities

Time	Teacher activity	Student activity	Resources
Before the activity	Prepare lists of questions and lists of answers. These can be related to other topics currently being studied. Each group of answers should be on a single topic (e.g. animals, composers). Each group of questions should have some from several topics (you may duplicate question sets). Each question should be on a separate piece of paper with space for the answer.		Question sheets, answer sheets.
5 mins	Discussion: what is the Internet? What does it do? Be sure to differentiate from the Internet World Wide Web as children often think these are the same things: compare websites, email, Skype, and messaging services such as Twitter and Facebook messages.		

(Continued)

(Continued)

Time	Teacher activity	Student activity	Resources
	Ask children to think about Internet-connected devices they use or have seen used. How are they connected? For each item, give a child a card showing that item. Draw out the different connection methods: wired network, WiFi, mobile.	Children will list devices such as phones, Playstations, tablets, laptops and TVs. Remind children that not all TVs are connected.	Picture cards of various devices.
5 mins	Split the children into groups, one for each set of questions. They will represent a person using a particular device to answer the questions. Specify whether the device uses a wired, WiFi or mobile connection.		
10 mins	Tell the children to answer their questions.	When told to do so, children take a question each to the relevant 'website', which are the answer sheets, write the answer on the slip and take it back to their device. The first group to answer all their questions is the winner. Children must walk at all times. Children may need to queue at a busy website. Children using a wired connection can hold the message in their hands; those using a WiFi connection carry it on the back of one hand; those using a mobile phone connection must carry it on their head. Every time they drop a message, they must stop and put it back before moving on.	
10 mins	Swap children around between devices (and connection types) and give them a new set of questions. Repeat the exercise so children can experience the different connection types.		
5 mins	Explain the presentation task. Show some models to give them some ideas.	Back in class, children have to come up with a way to present what they have found out about how the Internet works. They must choose an appropriate way of presenting their information.	

Scope for differentiation and extension

Support

Have a supply of ideas and pictures of connected devices for the 'brainstorming' part of the activity. Children may need prompting for devices or the connection type they use. The main questions to ask to distinguish connection types are whether it needs to be plugged in and whether it can be used far away from the house.

Children may become over-excited when moving around and getting access to the answers, so ensure that everyone remains safe and that all children have a fair turn at each point.

You may need to reinforce that the game is about showing the differences between connection types, not about finding winners and losers.

Stretch

To provide extra challenge, ask children to consider why we use slower and less reliable network connections and when each is appropriate. You might also ask them to consider how we could build reliable communication channels over unreliable connections (the communicating parties 'handshake' before and after messages to check that all parts were sent and delivered, resending as necessary).

Success criteria and assessment

If pupils have met the learning outcomes, they will be able to explain the different types of network connection and their relative advantages and disadvantages. They may also have learnt something about the question and answer topics.

Reflective questions

- Can you explain how the Internet works?

- What services do you use that share information over a computer network?

- Can you suggest a time when it would be appropriate to use a wired internet connection as opposed to a wireless internet connection?

- How do computer networks draw out the concepts and approaches of computational thinking?

Discussion

The key idea to draw out of this chapter is that data processing can be performed in many different ways, and using a digital computer or pen and paper are just two ways of doing it. Information can be physically stored and manipulated in many ways and this chapter has hopefully shown you some of them.

The first activity with sorting networks shows how an algorithm can be embodied in a physical arrangement. Sorting networks themselves aren't generally used in programming as each sorting network can only sort a particular number of items. However, with a fixed number of items and a highly parallel processor (such as a graphics card used as a processor), sorting networks can be efficient. A similar approach of parallel processing is used in modern artificial intelligence systems.

Another more physical sorting algorithm is the *pancake sort*, where a pile of pancakes of different sizes has to be put in order with the largest pancake at the bottom, the next largest above, and so on until the smallest pancake is on top. You can sort the pile by inserting a fish slice somewhere in a pile and flipping the top part of the pile. Repeated flips in the right places will eventually end up with the pile sorted. This could easily become a practical activity in a classroom, using paper discs of different sizes, and children investigating how many flips are needed to sort the whole pile.

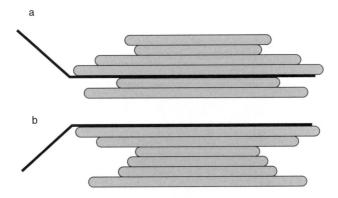

Figure 4.9 A step in a pancake sort

The fish slice is inserted under the fourth pancake in the pile (a) and the top portion of the pile is flipped over. This leaves the largest pancake on top (b). If, as the next step, the whole pile is flipped, the largest pancake will be on the bottom of the pile, which is where we want it. With more flips, we can sort the rest of the pile.

Computer networks are an obvious activity to move outside as networks themselves have a physical extent that maps to locations in a playground.

Understanding computer networks fits in the 'information technology' strand of the computing curriculum (alongside the 'computer science' and 'digital literacy' strands). Information technology is about the creative and productive use of computer systems in real-life situations. Therefore, an understanding of how computer networks operate is important when appreciating how computers can affect and benefit all our lives.

An important computational thinking feature that can be drawn out of studying computer networks is *abstraction*, where the details of how a message is passed from place to place are irrelevant to the outcome of a message being passed. Another computational thinking aspect is how computers themselves can *collaborate* to move messages around, and the unreliable nature of most networks requires computers to *debug* failed communication and *persevere* with sending the message in the face of failures.

Summary and Key Points

An unplugged approach that draws on drama and role-play allows children to build up an understanding of computational processes through kinaesthetic learning. This could be through an exploration of algorithms or data transmission.

Connectivity has become an integral part of 21st-century life. With this in mind, we need to be more and more aware about the technology behind networks and the Internet, so that we are able to best prepare ourselves and our pupils for a world where access to information is ubiquitous. The themes of this chapter are crucial for eSafety as well as for computing as they enable children to make informed decisions about what they are sharing online by knowing exactly what happens to their information or files.

This chapter not only discusses the different computer connections but also how data is represented and transmitted through a network. It explains the difference between wired, wireless and fibre connections, as well as how that data is transmitted using electrical pulses, radio waves and lights.

Useful links and further reading

DataGenetics on Amidakuji (using sorting networks backwards to scramble items) www.datagenetics.com/blog/may42014/index.html

TED Ed: How the Internet works in 5 minutes http://ed.ted.com/on/tdUFCocK

YouTube video explaining the role of IP address, URL, ISP, DNS www.youtube.com/watch?v=C3sr7_0FyPA

YouTube video explaining the use of packets when transferring information across the Internet **www. youtube.com/watch?v=WwyJGzZmBe8**

A definitive explanation of all things relating to the Internet **http://computer.howstuffworks.com/ internet/basics/internet.htm**

References

Department for Education (DfE) (2011) *Teachers' Standards*. Available from **www.gov.uk/government/ uploads/system/uploads/attachment_data/file/283566/Teachers_standard_information.pdf** (accessed 23 December 2015).

EMC (2014) The Digital Universe of Opportunities: Rich Data and the Increasing Value of the Internet of Things **www.emc.com/leadership/digital-universe/** (accessed 3 March 2016).

Chapter 5

CODE BREAKERS: DPEF CSFBLFST

Introduction

How many of us, when we were children, passed messages around the classroom to friends? How many of us had these messages read by our peers, or much to our embarrassment the teacher intercepted the message and read it (sometimes even out loud)? When I've asked pupils in my class these questions, I've found that more hands go up to the second question than the first. When I ask the same class of pupils who would want to be able to encrypt their messages to save any future embarrassment … every hand goes up!

Introducing the topic of code breaking and encryption to learners in this way creates an exciting hook and real-life context for learners to engage with this fascinating topic. It shows how pupils can, to quote from the National Curriculum, *use computational thinking and creativity to understand and change the world*. Encryption has played an important role throughout history (I give some examples below) and continues to be an important part of our lives. Every time we make a phone call, send an email or purchase something on the World Wide Web, these tasks depend on confidentiality and security. All organisations are required by law to look after and keep secure the data they store, and encryption plays a part.

Lesson ideas

There are several cipher methods we can use with pupils to encrypt and decrypt information in the classroom. I've described some of them in the '*A menu of ciphers*' section near the end of this chapter. You can use any of these ciphers for either of the 'Using ciphers' or 'Cracking ciphers' activities, though your students might find the later ciphers easier to understand after they've used the earlier ones.

Learning Outcomes

At the end of this chapter you should be able to:

- understand the importance of cryptography throughout history and in modern technology;
- explain that the process of encryption and decryption are algorithms;
- encrypt and decrypt messages using a range of simple ciphers.

Links to Teachers' Standards

The following Teachers' Standards are particularly relevant to this chapter:

TS1c Set goals that stretch and challenge pupils of all backgrounds, abilities and dispositions.
TS3a Have a secure knowledge of the relevant subject(s) and curriculum areas, foster and maintain pupils' interest in the subject, and address misunderstandings.
TS4b Promote a love of learning and children's intellectual curiosity.
TS4c Reflect systematically on the effectiveness of lessons and approaches to teaching.
TS5a Know when and how to differentiate appropriately, using approaches which enable pupils to be taught effectively.
TS6a Know and understand how to assess the relevant subject and curriculum areas, including statutory assessment requirements.
TS6b Make use of formative and summative assessment to secure pupils' progress.
TS6d Give pupils regular feedback, both orally and through accurate marking, and encourage pupils to respond to the feedback.

(DfE, 2011)

Links to National Curriculum Programmes of Study

Computing programme of study, Key Stage 2.

2.2 Use sequence, selection, and repetition in programs; work with variables and various forms of input and output.
2.3 Use logical reasoning to explain how some simple algorithms work and to detect and correct errors in algorithms and programs.
2.4 Understand computer networks, including the internet; how they can provide multiple services, such as the World Wide Web, and the opportunities they offer for communication and collaboration.
2.7 Use technology safely, respectfully and responsibly; recognise acceptable/unacceptable behaviour; identify a range of ways to report concerns about content and contact.

Need to know

Essential subject knowledge for teachers and pupils

In cryptography, a cipher is an algorithm for performing encryption or decryption. Like any algorithm, it has a series of well-defined steps that can be followed as a procedure.

Encryption is a process of transforming meaningful data, which cryptographers call 'plaintext', into indecipherable code, known as 'ciphertext'. Decryption is

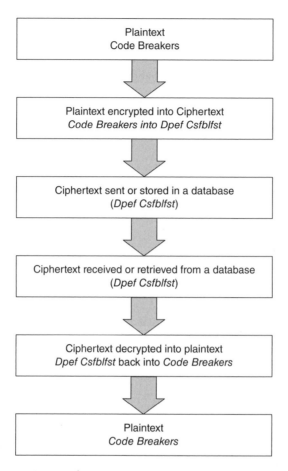

Plaintext
Code Breakers

Plaintext encrypted into Ciphertext
Code Breakers into Dpef Csfblfst

Ciphertext sent or stored in a database
(*Dpef Csfblfst*)

Ciphertext received or retrieved from a database
(*Dpef Csfblfst*)

Ciphertext decrypted into plaintext
Dpef Csfblfst back into *Code Breakers*

Plaintext
Code Breakers

Figure 5.1   Enciphering and deciphering

the process of turning the ciphertext back into the plaintext so that it can be understood by the intended viewer (see Figure 5.1). To be able to decrypt the ciphertext, the viewer must know the cipher method and have the key used to be able to view the plaintext.

Most cipher algorithms are well known so the strength of a cipher depends on how hard it is for an eavesdropper to find the right key. Good ciphers have lots of keys and don't provide clues to them in the ciphertext.

While we use the terms 'plaintext' and 'ciphertext', ciphers can and do encrypt all sorts of data, including text, numbers, sounds and images. This brings out an important point about how information is stored in a computer as just ones and zeros (binary). As all data looks the same at this low level, the same ciphers can be used to encrypt and decrypt the data, whatever its interpretation at a higher level.

There are many methods of encrypting information, some simple and straightforward, others more complex. In this chapter, we will look at a few simple but effective examples to use in the classroom with pupils, and look at how to break codes.

Cross-curricular links

Literacy
Writing messages, understanding the alphabet

Numeracy
Calculations in ciphers

History
Historical uses of ciphers

PHSE
Using ciphers for online safety

Design and Technology
Making cipher devices such as the Caesar cipher wheel

Computational thinking

The activities in this chapter develop a number of computational thinking aspects.

Algorithmic thinking

- Formulating instructions to be followed in a given order (sequence).

- Grouping and naming a collection of instructions that do a well-defined task to make a new instruction (subroutines, procedures, functions, methods).

- Creating algorithmic descriptions of real-world processes so as to better understand them.

Abstraction

- Reducing complexity by removing unnecessary detail.

- Choosing a way to represent an artefact, to allow it to be manipulated in useful ways.

- Hiding complexity in data, for example by using data structures.

Decomposition

- Breaking down artefacts into constituent parts to make them easier to work with.

Evaluation

- Assessing that an artefact is fit for purpose.

- Assessing whether an artefact does the right thing (functional correctness).

- Assessing whether the performance of an artefact is good enough (utility: effectiveness and efficiency).

- Comparing the performance of artefacts that do the same thing.

- Assessing whether an artefact is easy for people to use (usability).

- Assessing whether an artefact gives an appropriately positive experience when used (user experience).

- Stepping through processes or algorithms/code step-by-step to work out what they do (dry run/tracing).

Generalisation

- Identifying patterns and commonalities in artefacts.

- Adapting solutions, or parts of solutions, so they apply to a whole class of similar problems.

Unplugged Activity 1: Using ciphers

You are a secret agent who needs to send and receive classified messages to a fellow spy (a classmate). You need to investigate and carefully choose a cipher method to encrypt and decrypt your messages. Before you can send and receive your own classified messages you must return to spy training school.

Overview

There are a variety of ways of teaching how each algorithm for the ciphers work. My preferred method is to get pupils to break down the algorithms into smaller parts to make them easier to work with. Pupils do this by working their way through each algorithm (step-by-step) to work out what they do and then ask them to represent that as a sequence of instructions, using a standard notation, such as a flow diagram. They can then use these diagrams when attempting to crack the codes in Activity 2.

This same activity structure can be used with any of the ciphers described in the 'A menu of ciphers' section below, or any other cipher you may decide to use.

Age range

Beginning Key Stage 2 onwards. Caesar and pigpen ciphers might be usable by Key Stage 1 children.

Lesson plan

Learning outcomes

After this activity, students should be able to do and achieve these:

- I understand what is meant by the terms 'cryptography', 'encryption', 'decryptions', 'plaintext' and 'ciphertext'.
- I have a simple understanding of how encryption works and how it keeps personal and private information secure.
- I can encrypt and decrypt messages using a simple cipher.

Need to know

Cryptography is about keeping information secure so that even if it falls into the wrong hands it can't be understood. A cypher is a method for turning information from a form that people can read into one that people can't (called encrypting), and reversing the process (decrypting) when the right person wants to read it.

Key words and questions

cipher, plaintext, ciphertext, algorithm, key, password

Can you change how the algorithm operates by changing its inputs?

What's common between algorithms and what's different about each?

Activities

Time	Teacher activity	Student activity	Resources
10 mins	Lead a discussion about secrets and private communication. Who would want to keep secrets, and why? Who would want to find out someone's secrets? Emphasise that everyone has secrets and private information, such as a teacher's first name, or a student's address.	Pupil should brainstorm some things that might be secret but still need to be communicated or stored. Secret messages between spies, information people want to keep from criminals, and so on.	
25 mins	Give an example of a simple cipher, such as a Caesar cipher with a one-position shift. Show how to encipher and decipher messages with this cipher.	Pupils given a Caesar cipher wheel together with a word in ciphertext. Pupils should work out the position shift used, e.g. A become S. Pupils should then encrypt a message using a Caesar cipher with a position shift of their choice.	Pupils could make and use a cipher wheel. See the resources below.
25 mins	If there is time, explain to pupils how a range of ciphers work.	Pupils should encrypt and decrypt a number of simple messages using a range of ciphers.	For resources, refer to the Menu of ciphers below.

If pupils have seen and used a range of ciphers, they should evaluate the ciphers. Remember that good ciphers have lots of keys and don't provide clues to them in the ciphertext.

For each of the algorithms (cipher methods) pupils should think about:

- Does the algorithm do the right thing?

- How easy is the algorithm (cipher method) for people to follow?

- Is the algorithm (cipher method) fit for purpose? If not, why not?

Variations, differentiation and extensions

The choice of encryption method is up to you. You should choose one (or more) that is appropriate for your learners. You should use simpler ciphers with younger and less able pupils.

Some older and more able pupils will naturally want to investigate the ideas of using two ciphers, one after the other, to encrypt and decrypt their messages. This is possible and should be encouraged because it is only a matter of stepping through two algorithms, after the other.

Success criteria and assessment

The evaluation criteria are directly related to the learning outcomes:

- Are pupils able to explain how encryption keeps personal and private information secure?

- Are pupils able to successfully perform the algorithm to encrypt plaintext into ciphertext and vice versa to produce a different representation of a word or message?

- Are pupils able to evaluate and compare a range of ciphers they use?

However, you should be aware of the range of computational thinking skills that can be developed by using ciphers and you may want to modify how you lead this activity to emphasise different skills.

Unplugged Activity 2: Cracking ciphers

The term 'hacker' is a popular way to describe somebody who illegally tries to break the cipher method to access the plaintext, which it was not intended they should see. To develop pupils' computational thinking skills and associated attributes, it can be fun for pupils to try hacking an encrypted word.

Age range

End of Key Stage 2.

Learning outcomes

After this activity, students should be able to do and achieve these:

- I know what frequency analysis is and how it speeds up the code-breaking process of cracking a substitution cipher.
- I understand that personal and private information need to be kept safe and secure.
- I understand the need for and use of complex passwords and keep them secure.
- I can persevere and try to attempt to solve a problem with different methods.

Need to know

Computational thinking is a framework and not a recipe. It is a framework to encourage pupils to ask good questions. So it is important to encourage the pupils to ask appropriate questions about the cipher method.

I give some approaches to breaking simple ciphers below. These approaches are not foolproof algorithms: applying one approach will not always allow someone to read an enciphered message. Therefore, the cracking activity also develops the perseverance approach of computational thinking, encouraging pupils to keep trying to decipher messages even if their first attempt fails.

Key words

hacker, transposition, substitution, high-frequency, analysis

Activity

Begin by encrypting some words using one of the cipher methods pupils are familiar with. Give the pupils the word (either on individual sheets or using a board to show the whole class) and challenge them to decipher it.

You can provide suggestions on how to break ciphers by giving pupils the information below on cracking ciphers – even better would be to demonstrate breaking one piece of ciphertext in front of the pupils.

You may want to spend anywhere between 120 and 180 minutes on this activity, depending upon the age and ability of your pupils. It is impossible to allocate a length of time to each activity because this will depend upon the pupils' understanding of the concepts being taught and their problem-solving capabilities being applied.

When pupils have cracked the code, repeat the task but this time increase the single word to a short sentence and again tell them which cipher method you have used so that the pupils can consider the variables associated with that given method. Try using a different cipher method; this will help you assess the pupils' understanding of other cipher methods while reinforcing their computational thinking skills.

After one or two successful cracks, ask the pupils how they could work together to solve the task more quickly. How would they approach the task? What can they apply from the previous hacking tasks to this one?

Pupils should conclude that they should work as a team to reduce the amount of time it takes to crack the code, with some members trying some keys until they find one that works. This emphasises how tasks can be *decomposed* into smaller jobs, and how several tasks can be performed in parallel to improve overall performance.

Conclude this activity by leading a discussion with pupils. In this discussion it is really important that pupils apply what they have learnt about hacking of encrypted messages to their own computer behaviours, that is, understanding the importance of using complex passwords to keep their personal and private information secure from hackers. As part of this plenary ask pupils to consider:

- Do you trust your computer to keep things secret?

- Are there things that need to be kept secret or private?

- What things would you want encrypted?

Cracking substitution ciphers

One approach to cracking a cipher is to try every key and decipher the entire message for each key. This would be a very slow and tedious method of code breaking.

Instead, code breakers will often turn to frequency analysis to help them identify a pattern in the ciphertext. This is because certain letters and combination of letters

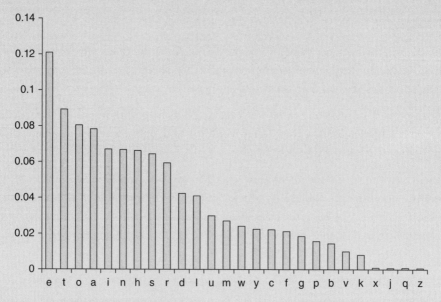

Figure 5.2 Graph to show frequencies of letter occurrences in English

occur with varying frequency. They are useful when a substitution cipher method has been applied to the plaintext.

The three most frequent letters in normal English are E then T and O. The title of this chapter contains the ciphertext 'Dpef Csfblfst'. Therefore, if you know that the cipher method was a substitution cipher, and the letter F appears three times in the ciphertext, it is likely that 'F' replaces one of these letters. If pupils know the message used a Caesar cipher, they can turn their cipher wheel to their guess, setting E to equal F, then use that to decipher a fragment of the message. If the deciphered message looks sensible, they can decipher the rest. If not, they can use a different setting and hence a different trial key, such as seeing if T is enciphered to F.

The same technique could be applied to the polybius square ciphertext '13 34 14 15 12 42 15 11 25 15 42 43'. The only difference when applying this technique is that instead of substituting the characters that appeared most in the ciphertext, pupils would substitute the high frequency number pair, that is, grid references.

Cracking transposition ciphers

If you use a transposition cipher, then it is important for pupils to think about what possibilities were available to you as the person encrypting the plaintext. Did you use a railfence method, and if so, how many rows could you have used given the length of the word? Or could it have been a route method, and again what are the likely grid dimensions?

Pupils will probably not think to collaborate with one another to complete the task. After a few minutes stop the pupils, again talk through what possibilities were available to you when encrypting the data. Through key questioning, encourage pupils to work as a team and divide the possible methods and associated variables between them to reduce the length of time it could take to crack the code.

Extension and differentiation

While pupils develop their hacking skills, it is important to tell the pupils which encryption method you used, otherwise it is too challenging for even the most able students.

Any easy way to adjust the difficulty in your choice of words: words with double letters, or phrases with one- or two-letter words are easier to crack, as the features of the message give people a place to start. Short messages and/or words with unusual letter combinations are harder (words like 'rhythm' are difficult).

When the pupils have undertaken and have cracked the code for a range of cipher methods, you can encrypt a short message in one of the cipher methods studied but this time you shouldn't tell them which method you used.

Success criteria and assessment

This activity promotes both the *concepts* of computational thinking and some of its *approaches*. Many of the concepts used and developed in this activity are the same as for Activity 1. However, cracking ciphers requires tenacity, allowing students to develop *perseverance* as they try out different guesses for the cipher keys, along with *debugging* and *tinkering* as they progressively refine their guesses.

Unplugged Activity 3: Encoding for transmission

Overview

Codes don't have to be used to conceal messages. They can also make it easier to transmit messages from place to place. Codes like semaphore or Morse code allow us to send messages across distances further than we can shout. Semaphore uses vision, while Morse code was invented for when telegraphs could only send a binary signal (the electrical switch was closed or open).

The Polybius cipher can be a good illustration of how changing the format of a message can make it easier to transmit. The Polybius square converts a message that uses 26 symbols in different combinations into one that only uses five symbols (typically the digits 1 to 5).

Age range

End of Key Stage 1 or beginning of Key Stage 2.

Learning outcomes

After this activity, students should be able to do and achieve these:

- Understand how a message can be represented in different ways.
- Transfer a message using semaphore and Morse code.
- Appreciate the historic importance of semaphore and Morse code.

Need to know

Computers use numbers to represent all the information they hold and process. The precise details of how information is represented is often not that important: we use *abstraction* to hide these details, instead concentrating on the information itself. We can take ideas from how semaphore, Morse and polybius codes change the representation of information to see the general *pattern* for changing representations as needed.

Key words

semaphore, Morse code, transmission, representation

Activities

Prior to the lesson search for or create A4 handout sheets that pupils can refer to, to send messages to a friend across the school hall or classroom.

Time	Teacher activity	Student activity	Resources
20 mins	Begin the lesson by introducing pupils to the idea of transmitting messages through semaphore.	Using the handouts, pupils should code and transfer simple messages using semaphore to one another, before their partner decodes them.	
20 mins	Then progress pupils to looking at and communicating via Morse code.	Using the handouts, pupils should code and transfer simple messages using Morse code to one another, before their partner decodes them.	
20 mins	Conclude this lesson by leading an investigation on how semaphore has been used through history	Ask pupils to investigate how Morse code has been used through history. Ask pupils to share any interesting facts they find out.	Information on Napoleon's *le systeme Chappe*.

Variations, differentiation and extensions

From my experience it is a good idea to use torches with pupils rather than sound devices because pupils struggle to make out what their partner is transmitting in Morse code.

If pupils are struggling with receiving Morse signals, the teacher may need to synchronise transmission and reception of messages by clapping a slow and steady beat.

Success criteria and assessment

The main success criteria for this activity are the ability to send and receive messages and the understanding that information can be represented in different ways. So long as the pupils understand the idea of changing representations, don't worry too much if they're unable to send long messages or even send any message reliably!

Taking it further...

... into networks

Returning to the hook for teaching encryption, that is, passing messages around the classroom, the pupils can consider encryption in the context of the everyday activities that depend on computer networks.

There are some great free unplugged resources published by the Digital Schoolhouse project called Networks and Communications Unplugged. These activities can be extended by eavesdropping on the messages being passed. From experience, revisiting these unplugged networking activities after completing the encryption activities described above can be a really valuable consolidation learning experience.

... into programming

You can bring computers into these activities. Spreadsheets can be used to encrypt, decrypt and crack messages. This can be a useful way to teach pupils Digital Literacy (functional IT skills). Using these tools highlights the value of computers at modelling good thinking and processing information effectively. You can also create encryption and decryption scripts in whatever programming environment the children are using.

Menu of ciphers

The activity resources included in the cipher overviews below are for illustration purposes. They can be used as standalone activities to develop the computational thinking skills needed before starting the spy challenges described above; alternatively, you could decide to combine your study of cryptography with data handling and solving a murder from the book *Certain Death* by Tanya Landman!

Substitution ciphers encrypt the plaintext by substituting each character of the alphabet for another character. There are a lot of substitution ciphers: I've described the Caesar, pigpen and polybius ciphers here. *Transposition* ciphers scramble the letters of the plaintext into an anagram. Reverse, railfence and column ciphers are simple examples.

The ciphers given below are generally in their simplest forms. Extension: use a keyword to scramble the ciphertext alphabet. This means the key has two parts: the keyword and the position of the wheel. This works best when the cipher is written out in columns of letters. The keyword is used to scramble the order of the letters on the ciphertext alphabet, so the keyword 'SECRET' would mean the ciphertext alphabet starts as 'SECRTABDFGHIJKLMNOPQUVWXYZ' before it is shifted.

Caesar cipher

In a Caesar cipher, each letter in the plaintext is substituted with the character that is one (or more) characters ahead of the character, that is, the character 'A' become the character 'B' and 'E' becomes 'F'. For example: 'Code Breakers' becomes 'Dpef Csfblfst'. The key for this cipher is the number of positions to move along when enciphering: a key of 14 would turn 'Code Breakers' into 'Qcrs Pfsoysfg'.

Pupils really enjoy making and using the Alberti cipher wheel (see Figure 5.3). It is a great way of supporting pupils with the substitution process when encrypting and decrypting messages. The wheel has two rotating discs, one inside the other, with the alphabet on both, enabling the substitution to take place. To encipher a letter, find the letter on the outer disc and write down the corresponding letter on the inner disc. Deciphering goes from the inner wheel to the outer wheel. For more able pupils, instead of using a cipher wheel, you could ask pupils to create a table with two columns to complete the substitution in the same way as the wheel. Presenting the substitution method in table format, provides the basis for modelling the cipher in a spreadsheet.

Making a paper cipher wheel: **https://inventwithpython.com/hacking/chapter1.html**

Student activity 1 resource (wheel): **www.digitalschoolhouse.org.uk/sites/default/ files/cms/docs/Clue%202%20-%20Code%20wheel.docx**

Student resource (activity): **www.digitalschoolhouse.org.uk/sites/default/files/cms/ docs/Clue%202.docx**

Resource answers: **www.digitalschoolhouse.org.uk/sites/default/files/cms/docs/ Clue%202%20Answers.docx**

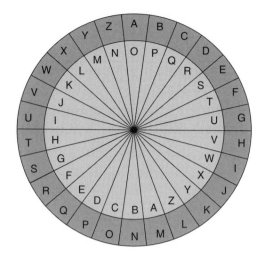

Figure 5.3 An Alberti cipher wheel

Pigpen cipher

The pigpen cipher is another type of substitution cipher (see Figure 5.4). The characters are encrypted by transforming them into symbols. These characters are placed into different grids. Each grid location, with different shapes inside, creates a unique set of symbols for the entire alphabet.

The ciphertext is a series of symbols. To decrypt the ciphertext the reader must know the combination of grids and shapes used and how the characters are allocated to the grids.

Student resource: **www.digitalschoolhouse.org.uk/sites/default/files/cms/docs/Clue%205.docx**

Resource answers: **www.digitalschoolhouse.org.uk/sites/default/files/cms/docs/Clue%205%20Answers.docx**

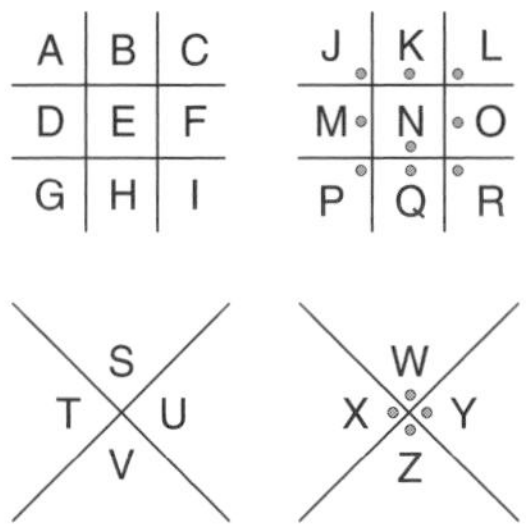

Figure 5.4 A pigpen cipher

Polybius square

A square grid of 5 by 5 is usually used. Although there are 26 characters in the alphabet, two letters are combined into a single cell of the table; usually this is 'I' and 'j'.

	1	2	3	4	5
1	A	B	C	D	E
2	F	G	H	I/J	K
3	L	M	N	O	P
4	Q	R	S	T	U
5	V	W	X	Y	Z

Figure 5.5   Polybius square

Alternatively, pupils could experiment with a 6 by 6 grid of 36 characters, which could enable them to include numbers (0–9) into the grid. The alphabet is allocated to the grid by first populating the first row, and then the second, and so on (see Figure 5.5). Each character in the alphabet is represented by its coordinates in the grid. For example, in a 5 by 5 grid the words 'Code Breakers' would become '13 34 14 15 12 42 15 11 25 15 42 43'.

To decrypt the ciphertext you need to know the grid used and if any (and which) of the letters of the alphabet have been combined into a single cell. Then use the grid references to turn the ciphertext into plaintext.

Student resource: **www.digitalschoolhouse.org.uk/sites/default/files/cms/docs/ Clue%201.docx**

Resource answers: **www.digitalschoolhouse.org.uk/sites/default/files/cms/docs/ Clue%201%20Answers.docx**

Reverse cipher

The reverse cipher method works by reversing the order of the string of characters in the plaintext to create the ciphertext. For example: 'Code Breakers' becomes 'srekaerB edoC'. This is possibly the simplest method encryption and the easiest method to crack. You can make it harder to crack by removing both the capitalisation of letters and the spaces. For example, 'Code Breakers' becomes 'srekaerbedoc'. Although this is an improvement, it is still relatively easy to crack. To make it a bit harder to crack by further disguising the plaintext, you can do this by grouping the ciphertext string of characters into groups. For example, 'Code Breakers' becomes 'sre kae rbe doc'. To support the pupils with this activity, it is best to give them centimeter squared paper to record the plaintext and ciphertext.

Student activity resource: **http://northofsepo.wikidot.com/activity:reverse-cipher**

Railfence cipher

When using this method, the message is split between two or more rows. To create the ciphertext you add the characters from the second row to the end of the first row.

C	o	d	e
b	r	e	a
k	e	r	s

Figure 5.6 A column cipher

For example, splitting a message over two rows would be: 'Code Breakers' becomes 'cdbekroeraes'. Splitting a message over three rows the ciphertext looks quite different with 'Code Breakers' becoming 'Ceee Obar drks'. To decrypt the ciphertext, to view the plaintext, you need to know the number of rows that the message was split over and then split the continuous string of characters into separate words.

Column cipher

This method involves creating a grid. Enter the message starting from the cell in the first row and column, entering the characters from left to right, before moving on to the second row (see Figure 5.6). The simplest way to encrypt the message and create the ciphertext is to start again at the top left-hand corner but this time move down the column before proceeding to the next column to create the anagram. To decrypt the ciphertext, you need to know the grid dimensions and the pattern used to encrypt the plaintext.

For instance, the phrase CODE BREAKERS, enciphered in a four-column grid, would become CBKOREDEREAS.

Student encryption activity resource: **www.youtube.com/watch?v=2_D2CkteKZI**

Student decryption activity resource: **www.youtube.com/watch?v=yNys2q9xmno**

Famous ciphers through the ages

The earliest ciphers found by archaeologists are hieroglyphics carved into Ancient Egyptian monuments (1900BC), then the Ancient Greeks were next to use ciphers to send military messages using the Polybius Square method (800BC), before Julius Caesar used a type of substitution cipher (50BC) which he tattooed into his messengers' heads before sending them to his military leaders.

In 1467 the Alberti Cipher was invented in Italy. It was a wheel with two rotating discs, one inside the other, to perform the substitution and encrypt letters in the alphabet. Then, in 1586, Mary Queen of Scots had her head chopped off because her communications with her followers were cracked, that is, her codes were broken, and a plot to assassinate Queen Elizabeth I was discovered.

We have all heard about the Enigma Code. It was originally intended to be used by finance and banking as a means of transferring money, but it was further developed and used by the German military to send classified information about military strategies during the Second World War. However, while the German military were trialling the Enigma Code, in 1932, a collaboration between the French Military Intelligence and Polish Cipher Bureau actually cracked the code.

Enigma design meant that there were 159 million million million possible settings to choose from and the cipher key was changed daily. During the Second World War, Alan Turing and his colleagues further developed this work and had some limited success. However, the team at Bletchley Park had to rely upon luck and incredible bravery because it wasn't until a German Enigma operator made a mistake, plus the daring capture of a book of cipher keys and an Enigma machine, were the Bletchley Park team able to regularly fully decrypt the messages. Because the teams at Bletchley Park were working around the clock and against the clock to crack the codes, they required a vast amount of computations to be carried out very quickly and humans were just too slow, so the Bletchley Park team built the first programmable, electronic computer to speed things up. It was called Colossus and was designed for the sole purpose of decrypting codes.

Modern-day encryption and code breaking using machines were developed at Bletchley Park during the Second World War. Therefore, in this chapter we have looked at how we can teach cryptography using a combination of unplugged (without computers) and plugged-in (with a computer) activities.

A useful slide deck for teaching the history of cryptography, which is described in the Overview section of this chapter, can be found at: **www.digitalschoolhouse.org.uk/ sites/default/files/cms/docs/6.%20Cryptography.pdf**

Reflective questions

- What is the role of the teacher in this chapter, through developing pupils' computational thinking capabilities and the pedagogical approaches described? How is it different from the traditional teaching pedagogy of ICT?

- How could the pedagogical approaches described in this chapter help to build confidence, resilience, communication and collaboration skills in pupils?

- Reflecting on the success criteria listed for each activity, did you see your pupils show the computational thinking techniques listed? Did your pupils demonstrate any others from the list published by Computing At School in the Computational thinking guidance for teachers document?

- How important is effective Assessment for Learning (AfL) in supporting pupils to develop their computational thinking capabilities? What does a pupil demonstrating 'computational thinking' skills look like? What behaviours will they be displaying during the lessons to help you to assess their learning?

- What are the challenges for classroom practitioners of pupils developing and applying creativity and computational thinking to help pupils take ownership of both the process they've gone through and the artefacts they produce?

Discussion

The encryption algorithms used here have been too weak for real uses for centuries, but the process of using them and understanding them allows pupils to explore many aspects of computational thinking, and how computers are a tool, rather than the focus of the learning. Once pupils understand a problem and how to solve it, they can move from the unplugged to the plugged, using computers and writing programs to run algorithms faster and on more data than is convenient for humans.

The Computer Science Teachers Association (CSTA) suggests that five dispositions are developed through computational thinking. From my classroom experience, I would agree that the following attitudes can be observed in learners.

Computing lessons

- Confidence in dealing with complexity.

- Persistence in working with difficult problems.

- Tolerance for ambiguity.

- The ability to deal with open-ended problems.

- The ability to communicate and work with others to achieve a common goal or solution.

Like any thinking skill, it is important to provide learners with opportunities to develop them. In the activities, I've suggested how to differentiate the tasks to support a range of pupil abilities. Gradually, as pupils progress through the activities in this chapter, it provides for more pupil-led learning but the key questions employed by the class teacher are pivotal to prompting and steering the pupils. When these computational thinking skills have been mastered, pupils should be able to successfully apply them to a range of problem solutions – not just encryption. Therefore, it is reasonable to suggest that there is an association between the pupil, the activity and the way in which the activity is presented to pupils by the class teacher.

Summary and Key Points

Although this chapter primarily deals with data representation and a range of simple algorithms to encrypt and decrypt text, it also highlights how this topic can be made fun and engaging for all pupils by adapting our pedagogical approaches to embed computational thinking through a constructionist approach to teaching. But it also highlights how relating the topic to the world that they, the pupils, understand, will serve as a hook to help them to understand the 'real world' and technologies that they take for granted. Pupils discover that all new technologies are iterations of previous technologies through investigating

(Continued)

(Continued)

semaphore and Morse code as a representation for transferring data and by looking at their historical relevance.

Finally, the pedagogical approach described through the activities presented in this chapter rely upon classroom practitioners developing both their subject content knowledge, but just as importantly, their pedagogical content knowledge which comes with experience and being a reflective practitioner.

Resources

Non-commercial

Crypto Corner (2016) Downloadable resources. Available from: **http://crypto.interactive-maths.com/downloadable-resources.html** (accessed 1 January 2016).

CS Unplugged (2015) Public Key Encryption. Available from: **http://csunplugged.org/public-key-encryption/** (accessed 1 January 2016).

CS Unplugged (2015) Cryptographic Protocols. Available from: **http://csunplugged.org/cryptographic-protocols/** (accessed 1 January 2016).

CS Unplugged (2015) Scout Patrol (Encryption). Available from: **http://csunplugged.org/scout-patrol-encryption/** (accessed 1 January 2016).

Digital Schoolhouse (2013) Cryptography: Secrets, secrets, secrets. Everyone has them! Available here: **www.digitalschoolhouse.org.uk/workshops/cryptography-secrets-secrets-secrets-everyone-has-them** (accessed 1 January 2016).

Digital Schoolhouse (2013) Step by step tutorials for modeling ciphers in a spreadsheet software. Available from: **www.youtube.com/results?search_query=mark+dorling+encryption** (accessed 1 January 2016).

Digital Schoolhouse (2014) Networks and communications unplugged. Available from: **http://community.computingatschool.org.uk/resources/2528** (accessed 1 January 2016).

Simkin. M (2006). Using spreadsheets to teach data encryption techniques. Available from: **www.aisej.com/doi/pdf/10.3194/aise.2006.1.1.27** (accessed 1 January 2016).

Commercial

Berry, M (2015) *Switched On Computing – Year 5 Unit 2: We are cryptographers*. London: Rising Stars.

Dorling, M and Rouse, G (eds) (2014) Compute-IT series (Teacher and Student books): Book 3 Unit 1: *Cracking the code*. London: Hodder Education.

Further reading

BBC (2013) Code breakers: Bletchley Park's Lost heroes. Details at: **www.bbc.co.uk/programmes/b016ltm0** (accessed 1 January 2016).

BBC (2013) Megabits: How computers changed the Second World War and all future digital communications. Available from: **www.bbc.co.uk/programmes/p011lptc** (accessed 1 January 2016).

Bletchley Park (2016) Learning at Bletchley Park. Available from: www.bletchleypark.org.uk/edu/ (accessed 1 January 2016).

Brennan, K and Resnick, M (2012) *New Frameworks for Studying and Assessing the Development of Computational Thinking.* Available from: http://web.media.mit.edu/~kbrennan/files/Brennan_Resnick_AERA2012_CT.pdf (accessed 1 January 2016).

Computing At School (2016) *Computational Thinking – A guide for teachers.* Available from: http://community.computingatschool.org.uk/resources/2324 (accessed 1 January 2016).

Computing At School (2016) QuickStart Computing, Section 4 Teaching. Available from: www.quickstartcomputing.org/secondary/section4.html (accessed 1 January 2016).

CSTA (2015) What does Computational Thinking develop in learners? Available from: www.csta.acm.org/Curriculum/sub/CurrFiles/CompThinkingFlyer.pdf

Department for Education (DfE) (2013) *National Curriculum in England: Computing programme of study.* Available from: www.gov.uk/government/publications/national-curriculum-in-england-computing-programmes-of-study/national-curriculum-in-england-computing-programmes-of-study (accessed 1 January 2016).

Department for Education (DfE) (2015) *Commission on Assessment Without Levels.* Available from: www.gov.uk/government/publications/commission-on-assessment-without-levels-final-report (accessed 1 January 2016).

Department for Education (DfE) (2015) *Government Response to the Commission on Assessment Without Levels.* Available from: https://www.gov.uk/government/publications/commission-on-assessment-without-levels-government-response (accessed 1 January 2016).

Dorling, M (2015) Networks and communications. In Williams, M (ed.) *Introducing Computing: A guide for teachers.* Oxford: Routledge, pp.107–120.

Dorling, M and Woollard, J (2015) Planning and assessing computing and computational thinking. In Allsop, Y and Sedman, B (eds) *Primary Computing in Action.* Woodbridge: John Catt Education, pp 163–184.

Landman, Tanya (2013) *Murder Mysteries 6: Certain Death.* London: Walker Books. www.walker.co.uk/Murder-Mysteries-6-Certain-Death-9781406347432.aspx (though you might have to go hunting for second-hand copies).

Ofsted (2015) *School Inspection Handbook from September 2015.* Available from: https://www.gov.uk/government/publications/school-inspection-handbook-from-september-2015 (accessed 1 January 2016).

Papert, S and Harel, I (1991) Situating constructionism. Available from: www.papert.org/articles/SituatingConstructionism.html (accessed 1 January 2016).

Royal Society (2012) Shut down or restart? Available from: https://royalsociety.org/topics-policy/projects/computing-in-schools/report/ (accessed 1 January 2016).

ScratchEd, How do I assess the development of computational thinking? Available from: http://scratched.gse.harvard.edu/ct/assessing.html (accessed 1 January 2016).

ScratchEd, Assessing development of computational practices. Available from: http://scratched.gse.harvard.edu/ct/files/Student_Assessment_Rubric.pdf (accessed 1 January 2016).

Selby, C and Woollard, J (2013) *Computational Thinking: The developing definition.* University of Southampton. Available from: http://eprints.soton.ac.uk/356481/ (accessed 1 January 2016).

Selby, C, Dorling. M and Woollard, J (2014) *Evidence of Assessing Computational Thinking*. Available from **http://eprints.soton.ac.uk/372409/1/372409EvidAssessCT.pdf** (last accessed 1 January 2016)

Wing, J (2006) Computational thinking, *Communications of the ACM*. Available from: **www.cs.cmu.edu/~15110-s13/Wing06-ct.pdf** (accessed 1 January 2016).

Wing, J (2011) Research notebook: Computational thinking – what and why? Available from: **www.cs.cmu.edu/link/research-notebook-computational-thinking-what-and-why** (accessed 1 January 2016).

References

Department for Education (DfE) (2011) *Teachers' Standards*. Available from **www.gov.uk/government/uploads/system/uploads/attachment_data/file/283566/Teachers_standard_information.pdf** (accessed 23 December 2015).

Landman, Tanya (2013) *Murder Mysteries 6: Certain Death*. London: Walker Books. **www.walker.co.uk/Murder-Mysteries-6-Certain-Death-9781406347432.aspx** (though you might have to go hunting for second-hand copies).

Chapter 6

MAGICIANS

Any sufficiently advanced technology is indistinguishable from magic.

Arthur C. Clarke (1973)

Introduction

'Pick a card, any card!' How often have you heard magicians say that? The normal routine is that you pick a card, the magician shuffles the deck, and abracadabra, reveals your chosen card. But behind this magic often lies some interesting maths and ideas used in computer science. It's hardly surprising then that some of the great magicians have also been computer scientists or mathematicians.

The link between magic and computing runs deep. All tricks consist of a secret method and a presentation. Unless both work, a magic trick will not be magical. Similarly, programs embody an algorithm (method) that must work and an interface (presentation) that must be easy to understand. The link between magic method and algorithm is not just a metaphor. Some magic tricks even use identical algorithms to computer algorithms. For example, one trick allows the magician to reveal that a card hidden in an envelope is the same as one selected by a member of the audience. The secret mechanism is just a search algorithm where the 'shuffles and deals' the magician makes secretly move the cards to eliminate all but the chosen one. If you think about a pack of playing cards as 52 distinct data elements the analogy between moving cards in a pack and data in a computer memory becomes a useful tool for explanations.

Similarly, the mechanism of another trick that allows a blindfolded magician to know exactly what card in a grid was turned over, is based on an algorithm used to correct the value of bits in a data package that may be corrupted in transmission. The pattern formed at the start is such that when you know the algorithm used, any change in one of the cards can be easily recognised.

This link makes magic a fun way to teach computing concepts: do a trick, challenge the class to work it out, explain the secret and the linked computing concepts. We have developed many activities using this format, illustrating concepts including algorithms, search, security, testing, proof and usability (Curzon and McOwan, 2008).

Magic provides an inspiring way to introduce computational thinking concepts too. Algorithmic thinking, logical thinking, evaluation, pattern matching, decomposition, abstraction, generalisation and the need for computational thinkers to understand people are there to explore in magic tricks, in a direct, hands-on way. The physicality allows engaging and fun explanations of the issues. It can be used to show what computational thinking is, separate from coding.

Writing instructions for how to do a trick involves algorithmic thinking, decomposition and abstraction in coming up with an appropriate way to describe them. You must specify the steps precisely and in the right order. They must work whatever happens.

Inventing new magic involves the same skills as inventing new algorithms. Good ideas from one trick can be reused to make another based on decomposition and generalisation, equivalent to code reuse in software. A different presentation can be developed, like changing a program's user interface.

Presentation matters in magic, giving a natural way to introduce the importance of understanding people in creating software. The same psychology makes a trick work well as makes a program usable. Tricks demonstrate how the design of a system can affect whether people make mistakes or not. Magicians control people's attention to make everyone make a mistake at the same time; a user interface needs to be designed to control their attention so they do not.

No one will do a trick that might not work in front of a live audience. Tricks give a way to introduce evaluation, showing how testing can be insufficient. Logical thinking can reduce the test cases needed to be sure a trick will work, or even prove the correctness of the algorithm.

Magic is thus a powerful way to introduce computational thinking. Creating a trick that you are sure works brings all the subskills into play. The tricks are easy and can be done with an audience that has no computing experience at all.

Not only computer scientists but also magicians need to develop computational thinking skills. Programmers really are wizards!

Learning Outcomes

At the end of this chapter you should be able to:

- explain the link between computational thinking and magic;
- explain computational thinking concepts using magic;
- use tricks to teach computational thinking skills.

Links to Teachers' Standards

The following Teachers' Standards are particularly relevant to this chapter:

TS1 Set high expectations which inspire motivate and challenge pupils.
TS3 Demonstrate good subject and curriculum knowledge.
TS4 Plan and teach well-structured lessons.

(DfE, 2011)

Unplugged Activity 1: Invisible palming

Overview

You do a magic trick that involves invisibly moving a card from one pile to another. You show the audience they can do it themselves – even when they still don't know how it works – if they follow the steps exactly. After challenging the audience to work out how it is done, you explain the trick and the link to computing. In doing so you introduce the idea of an algorithm in a fun way, showing how algorithms are a series of steps that, if followed precisely, lead to something being guaranteed to happen – even if the person (or computer) following the algorithm doesn't know what they are doing.

Tell the class you are going to show them a magic trick and teach them how to do it. Along the way they will learn something about how computers work (including gadgets like their mobile phone). Get a volunteer to come to the front and have everyone else gather round the table so that they can see (see References: Invisible Palming Activity).

Need to know

Teachers need to understand what an algorithm is and the basics of computational thinking, particularly decomposition and abstraction.

The trick

Ask a volunteer to put their hands as though playing the piano, so fingers and thumbs touch the table. While everyone chants the magic words 'Two cards make a pair' throughout, place two cards together between two of their fingers. Do the same with another pair, placing them between different fingers. Do this repeatedly until one card is left. Place the last card between the last fingers/thumb saying 'and one left over'.

Take the first pair back, starting two separate piles with them. Keep taking pairs, putting the cards on the two piles until only the single card is left with the chant said continually. Say: 'We have one left over. It could go on either pile. It's your choice.'

The volunteer adds the extra card to a pile. Explain you will invisibly move the extra card from one to the other. Place your hand over the pile with the extra card. Rub it to 'make the card go invisible'. Lift your palm and show that it has 'invisibly stuck to your hand'. Move your hand to the other pile and tap it to 'make the card drop'. Announce the card has moved.

To prove it, take the pile that had the extra card and count the pairs into a new neat pile – 'Two cards make a pair. Two cards make a pair…' The extra card has disappeared. Where to? Repeat with the other pile. Amazingly, after the pairs have been counted out an extra card is left. It has moved piles!

Now tell the class that they can do magic too. Give them cards to do the trick in pairs. Talk them through the steps without telling them how it works. To their surprise, even though they don't know how they did it, they also managed to move the card. Encourage them to experiment to work it out.

Give the children a chance to suggest how the trick works, then explain it together with the linked computing.

The explanation

A magician calls this a self-working trick. It always works if you follow the steps exactly. It appears magical because you have confused everyone. The secret is, in fact, $7 + 1 = 8$. There are 15 cards. They believe adding the last card to a pile adds an extra odd card. It actually makes up the last pair, making an odd pile even. After dealing out the pairs there are 7 cards in each pile. Whichever pile gets the extra card becomes 8: 4 pairs so no 'extra' card. The other pile will be left with 7 cards, 3 pairs with one left over that you pretend has magically moved. Nothing has to move!

To demonstrate this, repeat the trick explaining it, but laying out the cards so all can be seen and counted. Match the pairs and when you add the last card point out it has made up the last pair.

What does this have to do with computing? Well, a self-working trick is just an algorithm, as is a computer program. An algorithm is a series of steps to follow that, if followed in the right order, will lead to a guaranteed effect: here a magical effect; for a program, whatever it is supposed to do. For both, the instructions have to be precise and cover all eventualities.

A simplified version of the algorithm is:

1. count out the pairs;

2. put them into 2 piles adding the extra card to one pile;

3. pretend to move the card;

4. reveal the card has moved.

These steps can then be decomposed. For example, to count out the pairs:

1. have a volunteer place their hands on the table as though playing the piano;

2. do 7 times:

   a. Place 2 cards between the volunteer's fingers;

   b. Say 'Two cards make a pair';

3. place the final card between the remaining finger and thumb.

The other steps can be expanded similarly.

Programs are written in programming languages: languages computers can follow. Tricks are written in English for a person to follow. Both have to be precise enough that whoever is blindly following them will get the effect even if they have no idea what they are doing. Computers are just machines so can only blindly follow instructions.

A magician who invents new tricks is creating algorithms. A programmer writing a program is doing the same. They are both using computational thinking skills, in this case algorithmic thinking. Algorithmic thinking is what you do when you think up the series of steps that will have the right effect. You are also doing it when you check all the details to make sure it always works. Algorithmic thinking also involves writing instructions really precisely so that there is no confusion about what to do.

Computational thinking features developed

This trick introduces algorithmic thinking, decomposition and abstraction skills in writing instructions in detail at a suitable level of abstraction. Evaluation and logical thinking are needed to check the trick always works.

Cross-curricular links

Numeracy

- counting, understanding odd and even numbers

Literacy

- writing clear, concise instructions for a purpose and giving clear explanations

Science

- setting up simple practical enquiries

Age range

Key Stage 2.

Lesson plan

Learning objectives

After this activity, students should be able to:

- explain what is meant by an algorithm;
- write an abstract version of an algorithm;
- decompose an algorithm in to separate parts.

Key words and questions

algorithm – a precise sequence of instructions for getting something done

abstraction – hiding detail

decomposition – breaking down a problem into smaller manageable parts

user interface – software that defines how the user interacts with the program

- What do magic tricks have to do with computing?

- What's the best way to teach a friend to do the trick?

- Can you write the algorithm given in less steps? What do you want to change and why?

- Does your algorithm contain all the parts it needs? How can you be sure?

- How can you test your algorithm works correctly?

Activities

Time	Teacher activity	Student activity	Resources
10 mins	Introduction. Do trick.	Watch the trick, one volunteer.	Pack of cards, table with mat
5 mins	Talk students through steps.	Do trick in pairs.	
20 mins	Encourage scientific enquiry. Support.	Experiment to work out mechanism.	15 cards per pair of students
10 mins	Demonstrate how it works and conclude.	Students gather round to watch	

Success criteria and assessment

Students can:

- explain what an algorithm is in terms of a magic trick and the link to programs;

- use logical and scientific thinking to work out how a trick works;

- explain how it works;

- write precise instructions for others to follow;

- decompose the main steps, substituting new steps for old.

Scope for differentiation and extension

Short version

For a simpler version, rather than have the students work the trick out, just have your volunteer switch to being the magician after they have said they don't know how it works.

Then emphasise the link to computers being able to do things even though they don't know what they are doing or why – just blindly following instructions.

Writing algorithms

Everyone writes their own crib sheet (algorithm) to follow at home. Test the instructions, checking no steps are missed and everything is in the right order. What is the right level of detail for a crib sheet to remember the main steps and to learn the trick from scratch? This is a gentle introduction to working with abstraction, what's important and needs to be considered, and what isn't.

Inventing variations

In groups invent new versions for pretending to move the card. Use magical props (handkerchiefs, wands, hats). Explore how decomposition allows details to be changed leaving the overall effect.

Extension questions

Would this trick work if it used more or less cards? Would it become too simple or too complicated?

Unplugged Activity 2: Turning the page on book magic

Overview

You take a book that involves witches or wizards: *The Wizard of Oz* or *Macbeth* for example, and demonstrate how magic has seeped into the words of such books over the ages. We will use Shakespeare's *Macbeth* to illustrate, but just about any book will do: choose one that is appropriate to the class and ideally one they will recognise. It is most magical if the first sentence is quite long. A volunteer picks a word then, letting the book direct them, they end up with a word no one could have known, but that matches your hidden prediction (*Computational Thinking*: *Magical Book Magic*).

In exploring how the magic works, you learn about computational thinking, especially the importance of evaluation to algorithmic thinking. You explore the need to test algorithms and why testing ideally needs to be exhaustive, but how with some logical thinking less work needs to be done when testing. The magic trick shows how computer scientists, engineers and magicians have to evaluate their algorithms thoroughly.

Need to know

The teacher needs to understand what an algorithm is, what testing is, how programs are tested by trial and error. They need to understand how to create appropriate diagrams, based on their chosen text, to allow the proof to be worked through by the class.

The trick

Give a volunteer a pen and clipboard with the opening lines of *Macbeth* written out. The last part of the quotation is in italics.

When shall we three meet again

In thunder, lightning, or in rain?

. . . .

When the hurlyburly's done,

When the battle's lost and won.

That will be ere the set of sun.

Where the place?

Upon the heath.

There to meet with Macbeth.

Placing their hand on the book, they read the passage 'drawing on its magical power'. Words spoken, magic swirling, they pick a word from the first sentence (before the dotted line). Now the magic of the book controls them, jumping from word to word, guided by the words themselves. Suppose they choose 'again'. They say it then circle it. They count the number of letters in the word chosen (5 for 'again'), counting forward that many words (ignore punctuation). Counting 5 words on takes them to 'in'. They circle it and do the same from there. From 'in' they would count 2 words to land on 'When', and so on. They keep doing this, *from wherever they start*, until they land on an italic word. They then stop and announce the word. Confirm with them that their original word was their own free choice and that they had no idea where they would finish – no one knew.

Explain you were also guided by the book, and placed an envelope with a prediction in, under the paper they have been writing on. They open it. Inside is the word 'HEATH': remarkably the same as the italic word they ended up at.

This is another self-working trick, an algorithm for magic, because it always works if you follow the steps. It always works with the words from *Macbeth*. Amazingly, it works with any book about magic. Try it with the words from the start of *The Wonderful Wizard of Oz*. Choose a word from its first sentence, follow the steps, stopping when you first land on a word in the third sentence. It will be 'FOUR'. Try *The Cat in the Hat*. The first word you land on on the second page will be 'SAT'. It actually works with just about any writing, though sometimes the sentence to be italic is further on. Powerful, deep magic? No. It's a simple, if surprising, computational property of books.

Explanation

We've claimed the trick always works. Do you believe us enough to try it yourself on a live audience? How can you be sure? You need to evaluate the algorithm. Try it a couple of times. Does that give you convincing enough evidence it always works? What if they pick a word you didn't try? You have no idea whether it works for that one and will look silly if your prediction is wrong.

The class should test it works for every word in that first sentence. It helps to switch to a simpler book like *The Cat in the Hat* first. Give everyone a copy of the first sentences, and have them work out whether it does *always* work (see the example for *Macbeth* in Figure 6.1). Make sure they check their work really, really carefully. If anyone ends up on a different word, go back and check it with them and highlight how important it is to take care but also double-check results.

Have them work out how they might reduce the testing effort, while still being sure it always works. Once you hit any word already tested you don't need to follow that trail again further, for example.

Talk about algorithms, evaluation, testing programs and the importance of doing it thoroughly. Tell stories about software that *must* work every time so be thoroughly tested.

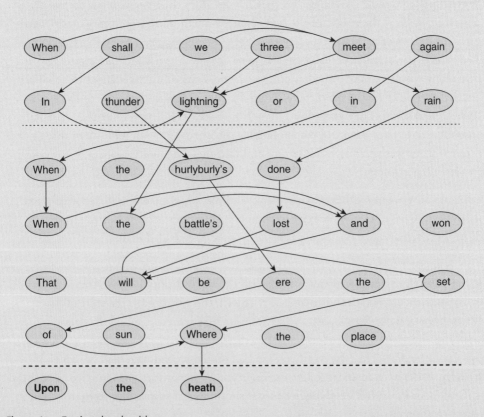

Figure 6.1 Testing the algorithm

I recently flew to Lapland to search for Father Christmas. The pilot announced that as it was foggy, she was letting the computer (an algorithm) land the plane for her.

Of course you don't need to know why the trick works to be able to do it – it's an algorithm and that is the point. What is happening is that once two paths meet they don't split. As the words are generally short and of different lengths, paths quickly meet up by chance. The amazing thing is actually not that so many writers have written books so that we can predict a word, but that any might have managed to write a book where we can't.

Computational thinking features developed

This activity develops evaluation skills around testing, why it needs to be exhaustive and also how logical thinking reduces the work.

Cross-curricular links

Numeracy

- counting

Literacy

- reading and writing passages

- seeing books in an exciting way that encourages an interest in words

- writing a special kind of story 'free from magic'

Science

- setting up simple practical enquiries

Age range

Key Stage 2.

Lesson plan

Learning objectives

After this activity, students should be able to:

- explain the importance of evaluating algorithms thoroughly;
- evaluate simple algorithms, using logical thinking;
- explain the importance of testing software.

Key words and questions

evaluation – checking an algorithm works

testing – running a program to check it gives the right result

proof – using logical thinking to be sure something is true

- Name books about witches, wizards or other creatures with magical powers. Does anyone know of books that had magical powers?

- What happens if there are lots of very short or very long words in the story? Does the trick work?

- Can you rewrite the story so that the chosen word is reached sooner? What did you have to do to the words to make this happen?

- Will this trick work with numbers instead of words? If so, what range of numbers would you use and why?

Activities

Time	Teacher activity	Student activity	Resources
15 mins	Introduction. Do the trick.	Watch the trick, one volunteer.	Book, pen, clipboard, sheet with passage, prediction in envelope.
20 mins	Observation and support.	Test the trick on a simple book and other books for those who finish quickly.	One copy of passage per child, pens.
15 mins	Overview.		

Success criteria and assessment

Students can:

- explain what an algorithm is in terms of a magic trick and the link to programs;

- use logical thinking to work out how a trick works;

- explain how it works;

- explain why testing an algorithm a few times does not show it always works;

- test it exhaustively, showing attention to detail;

- explain why evaluation of algorithms is important.

Scope for differentiation and extension

Create your own version of the trick
Each student creates a version of the trick from their favourite book. They write out the first few sentences, then follow the paths from all words in the first sentence noting

where they join. If more than one path is left, add more sentences. The line is drawn after the first sentence; the bold sentence is the first full sentence after they join up.

Write a story the magic doesn't work for

Does the trick work with absolutely any writing? Can they come up with a story it didn't work for? One way is for every word to be the same length: 'The cat ate the rat but was sad…' Have them try and write a short story of only three-letter words, checking the trick doesn't work.

Exhaustively test a program

With classes that have started programming, explore what it means to exhaustively test simple programs. How much testing is enough? Can logical thinking reduce the number of tests?

Unplugged Activity 3: The teleporting robot

Overview

You show a jigsaw of robots. There are 17 but a moment later one has disappeared! This introduces a simple design principle 'Keep it simple, stupid'. It shows how important it is to take human limitations into account when coming up with solutions to problems.

Need to know

Teachers need to be confident about how the jigsaw is manipulated, so some practice should be undertaken. Also, teachers should be sure they can indicate both the impossibility of the original robot vanish, and indicate the clues in the design that will help pupils discover the technique.

The trick

Explain you have a magical jigsaw of robots. The class must help work out which one disappears and where they are going!

Take a large version of the jigsaw illustrated in Figure 6.2 and follow the five steps below.

1. Put the pieces together as shown.

2. Count the robots. There are 17.

3. Swap the two pieces in each of the top two rows.

4. Count them again. There are 16!

5. Ask: which robot disappeared?

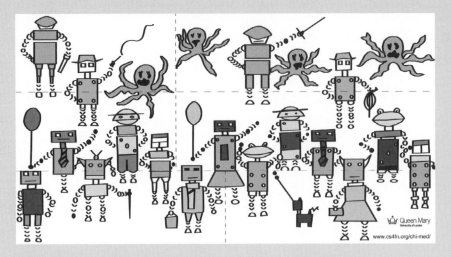

Figure 6.2 Disappearing robots

(Note you can download the robots image used in this activity for free from **www.cs4fn.org/magic/teleportingrobot.php**; see also References)

Everyone can make the magic work – even without knowing how it works – so this can be used to demonstrate what is meant by an algorithm. Go back and forth a few times and see if anyone has ideas as to what is going on. Give everyone a copy and let them try to puzzle it out, testing their theories. The one on the end loses and gains the top of his head! This is something to do with it, but it doesn't explain a whole robot disappearing! If a theory is a specific robot disappears, they should put their finger on it and follow it. Both parts are still there. Suggest they try and simplify things – are any robots definitely not involved? The top 4 don't change, just move, so the top of the jigsaw can be discarded: 13 robots now become 12. Simplifying problems is important in, e.g. debugging.

Explanation

Only explain the secret once everyone agrees to abide by the magician's code not to give it away. It isn't one robot that disappears, they all squash together. As they swap pieces, they all get taller. As you move along the chain of swaps the amount swapped gets larger until eventually a whole body is moved leaving nothing behind. The chain starts with the one on the end. It ends with a robot in the middle that completely moves position as it is all above the cut.

It is easier to see if we simplify things again. In Figure 6.3 we have replaced the robots with lines representing their height. Lines that swap pieces with each other are adjacent. Cut along the diagonal line. Count the lines, then slide the pieces up the diagonal making lines match again. Count the lines: one has disappeared. At one end a line has no part below the diagonal, at the other is a line that has no part above. Each line loses a little, but gains a larger piece, and so is taller, just like the robots.

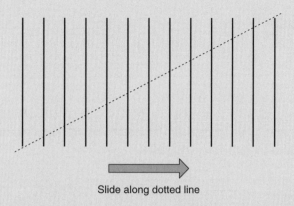

Slide along dotted line

Figure 6.3 Simplification of the robots trick

This shows that some things are so complicated our brains can't cope. We can't see what is happening even when it is before us. The same applies to gadgets. Show the Microwave Racing Video (see References) to illustrate how different designs can make a gadget easier or harder to use.

Simple elegant user interfaces can often be far easier to use than complicated ones. TV remote controls are a good example of something made too complicated: get them in an odd mode and even simple things become apparently impossible. For a TV it might mean you miss the start of *Dr Who* because you couldn't get it in the right mode and so change channel. That's just (very) irritating! If an A&E doctor has hooked you to a life-saving machine and is trying to set it going, it matters an awful lot that they aren't struggling to get it in the right mode because it is badly designed.

The jigsaw design is more complicated than the lines. The presentation makes the difference. Even though logically the same thing is happening, with the lines it is fairly easy to *see* what is happening. With the robots it is impossible – our brains can't process it all.

Magicians try to design systems like the robot version of the puzzle that forces people to struggle; software engineers should try to design systems like the lines that are easy to follow. Unfortunately, many software engineers do not think about people and unwittingly create systems too much like magic! An important interaction design principle is to keep things simple – aim to design clear, uncluttered interfaces. The reason many everyday gadgets are so hard to use is because the emphasis has been on adding features that are never used, each making the interface more complex, rather than focusing on making the core task easy to achieve well. Successful computational thinking takes human limitations into account.

Computational thinking features developed

This activity develops algorithmic thinking and logical thinking, as well as introducing a new aspect of evaluation: human limitations must be taken into account.

Cross-curricular links

Numeracy

- counting

Design and Technology

- design for a context, making products suitable for their intended users and using simple design criteria to help develop ideas

Science

- setting up simple practical enquiries

Art and Design

- the extension involves drawing a personal version of the trick

Age range

Key Stage 2.

Lesson plan

Learning objectives

Students can:

- explain what an algorithm is;
- explain why design must take human limitations into account;
- explain why gadgets can be hard to use and evaluation is important.

Key words and questions

user interface – the software used to interact with a program

- Name gadgets that some people (parents, grandparents) find hard to use. What makes them so difficult?

- Why is good design important to computer software?

- Can you create your own version of the puzzle? What shapes would you use and why?

- Could you make a puzzle where more robots vanish? What would be the problems in designing that?

Activities

Time	Teacher activity	Student activity	Resources
10 mins	Introduction. Demonstrate trick.	Watch the trick.	Large version of jigsaw.
20 mins	Encourage, support.	Explore how the trick works.	A4 version for each person in the class.
5 mins	Play video	Watch video.	Microwave racing video.
10 mins	Explain how it works and the design principle.		Line version of puzzle.

Success criteria and assessment

Students can:

- use observation and logical thinking to find clues as to how the puzzle works;
- explain why keeping interfaces simple matters;
- explain why gadgets can be hard to use.

Scope for differentiation and extension

Create your own magical jigsaw

Draw new versions of the jigsaw to make other things disappear (e.g. flowers) by following our draw-the-magic algorithm (Creating a Vanishing Creature Puzzle). This takes attention to detail. More simply, draw a version with lines following the pattern of the robot jigsaw.

Design a gadget

Design the front panel of a child's alarm clock. What buttons and controls are needed and can it be designed in a way that is really simple to understand and use?

Reflective questions

- How close is the link between a good self-working magic trick and a good piece of software?

- When people can't use a gadget are they stupid or could the technology be better designed?

- What parts of a computer program are the most important and why?

- In what areas is safety critical software used, and how can it be made as safe as possible?

Discussion

In this chapter we have shown how self-working magic tricks provide a useful similarity to well-designed computer programs. We have stressed the importance of both understanding the algorithm and, as importantly, the human being using the software.

Well-designed programs are like magic tricks: both the algorithm and presentation must be right for both. These unplugged activities provide engaging hooks to draw pupils into wanting to find out more about the tricks, and so the computational thinking principles behind them. Poor human factors often make software difficult to use, leading to people thinking 'I can't use technology'. These activities introduce usability problems that can arise, and issues that need to be considered for good software design through the direct analogy of a good trick presentation. Magic tricks also highlight the importance of evaluation with students able to undertake fun, practical examples of testing themselves. This is vital but often neglected. The tricks provide fertile ground for cross-curricular follow-on and give students the chance to explore their creativity in developing variant tricks, introducing the important principle of generalisation and component reuse.

Summary and Key Points

Magic provides a fun and engaging structured process to learn about computational thinking including algorithmic thinking, evaluation, abstraction, decomposition, logical thinking and the importance of understanding people. It uses a physical hands-on system to support enquiry-based learning. Students also learn magic tricks they can perform to entertain friends and family, giving them a useful new social skill.

Resources and further reading

Resources for teachers around magic and other unplugged activities are available from Teaching London Computing (**www.TeachingLondonComputing.org**) funded by the UK Department for Education, Mayor of London and support from Google.

Resources for students including three computer science magic books are available from Computer Science for Fun: (**www.cs4fn.org/magic/**) with support from EPSRC.

References

Baum, Frank L (1900) *The Wonderful Wizard of Oz*. London: Wordsworth Classics.

Computational Thinking: Magical Book Magic. Available from **http://teachinglondoncomputing.org/resources/computational-thinking-magical-book-magic/**

Creating a vanishing creature puzzle. Available from www.cs4fn.org/magic/drawingcreatures.php

Curzon, P and McOwan, PW (2008) Engaging with Computer Science through Magic Shows. In Proceedings of the 13th ACM SIGCSE Annual Conference on Innovation and Technology in Computer Science Education, pp179–183. ACM. 2008.

Department for Education (DfE) (2011) *Teachers' Standards*. Available from **www.gov.uk/government/uploads/system/uploads/attachment_data/file/283566/Teachers_standard_information.pdf** (accessed 23 December 2015).

Dr Seuss (1957) *The Cat in the Hat*. London: HarperCollins.

Microwave Racing Video: Available from **http://teachinglondoncomputing.org/resources/inspiring-unplugged-classroom-activities/microwave-racing-video/**

Shakespeare, William *Macbeth*. London: Wordsworth Classics.

The Invisible Palming Activity. Available from **http://teachinglondoncomputing.org/resources/inspiring-unplugged-classroom-activities/the-invisible-palming-activity/**

The Teleporting Robot: Available from **http://teachinglondoncomputing.org/resources/inspiring-unplugged-classroom-activities/the-teleporting-robot-activity/**

Chapter 7

GAMERS

The role of the teacher is to create the conditions for invention rather than provide ready-made knowledge.

Seymour Papert

Introduction

Teaching young learners about abstract principles of computing can be a very challenging task. A lack of sufficient technology in schools also compels us to think of alternative methods of teaching. In this chapter we will focus on how computing concepts can be introduced through playing card and board games. First, we would like to discuss briefly the relationship between play and games.

Championed by John Dewey (1938) and developed by Jean Piaget and Barbel Inhelder (1969), constructivism is a learning theory that focuses on knowledge and explores how people learn. Piaget (1954) suggests that play allows children to rehearse their newly developed concept to fit within what they already know (assimilation). They experiment with new activities and ideas that enable them to build new mental models through imitation (accommodation). Games as an engaging and interactive medium can potentially provide a space for repeated problem-solving practice. This approach is also well inclined with the constructivist perspective, which holds that people construct meaning through their interactions and experiences in social environments. According to Piaget (1970), children learn when they are actively involved in the process. This is very similar to the experiential learning perspective, which suggests that students learn better when they actively construct meaning by exploring and experiencing authentic contexts for themselves. Games provide learners with an authentic task, which engages them in problem solving. Games also provide experiential learning spaces, where learners examine and reflect on the situation using resources available in the service of complex problem solving. Another benefit of learning through game playing is the opportunity for collaborative learning. When children play multiplayer games, they take part in collaborative activities, where they can exchange ideas, develop communication skills and appreciate each other's perceptions.

Vygotsky's constructivism (1978) is known as social constructivism because he stressed the importance of the social context and culture within the learning process. He described learning as a collaborative activity and explained the significance the role of history and the social environment bear in acquiring new knowledge. Learning takes place when children interact with the social environment and internalise their experience. Vygotsky (1978) suggests that cognitive development is limited to a certain range at a particular age; however, with the help of social interaction, such as assistance from a teacher, students can understand concepts that they cannot know on their own.

Through game playing we can teach learners about vital computing concepts. Students learn to design algorithms to achieve a specific outcome and practise to determine the outcome of conditionals. They use different programming commands to create a sequence to complete a task or use Boolean logic to solve a problem. This helps learners to actively monitor their own learning and see the outcome of their program or solution immediately. Working in pairs or groups, they form their understanding through interactions with others.

Computational thinking through board games

If designed correctly, board games can provide a context for children to develop computational thinking skills. Based on the ability to think logically, algorithmically and recursively, computational thinking involves knowledge of the fundamentals of computing such as algorithm, iteration and generalisation. It also includes logical reasoning, problem decomposition, testing, debugging and visualisation skills. Developing these skills enables students to represent and solve problems computationally in any discipline and daily life.

In a computer game, rules are executed and enforced by the game itself whereas in a board game players follow a set of rules with a few decision points and use specific conditions to make decisions. Using the board and card games examples provided in this chapter, players design algorithms to reach their goal or accomplish a task and visualise the outcome while working on their sequence by placing programming cards on their sequence cards. They test if their program works by moving their character on the game board and debug it if there are errors. This can be seen as a continuous problem-solving process. In this process, players tackle problems by breaking them into smaller parts and using solutions for similar tasks or problems. They use repeat functions to create loops where appropriate and receive points as a reward for completing the task.

This chapter will explore how we can support pupils developing computational thinking with a focus on conditional statements and Boolean logic through board and card games.

Three activities are presented:

- *Space Race:* Learning about conditional statements through playing the 'Space race' board game.
- *Can you find the criminal?:* Learning about Boolean logic through solving puzzles based on detective stories.
- *Coding with cards:* Learning about 'If' and 'else' statements through card games.

Learning Outcomes

At the end of this chapter you should be able to:

- develop knowledge and understanding of programming concepts such as: algorithms, conditional, evaluation, logic;
- design an unplugged gaming activity to teach children about computing concepts;
- gain an understanding of how to assess children's learning in computing.

Links to Teachers' Standards

The following Teachers' Standards are particularly relevant to this chapter:

TS1a Establish a safe and stimulating environment.
TS1b Set goals that stretch and challenge pupils.
TS2e Encourage pupils to take a responsible and conscientious attitude of their own work and study.
TS3a Have a secure knowledge of the relevant subject(s) and curriculum areas.
TS4e Contribute to the design and provision of an engaging curriculum.

(DfE, 2011)

Links to the National Curriculum Programmes of Study

Key Stage 1

- Understand what algorithms are
- Create and debug simple programs
- Use logical reasoning to predict the behaviour of simple programs.

Key Stage 2

- Design, write and debug programs that accomplish specific goals
- Use sequence, selection, and repetition in programs
- Use logical reasoning to explain how some simple algorithms work and to detect and correct errors in algorithms and programs.

(DfE, 2013)

Key terms

Algorithm: An algorithm is a set of precise instructions to solve a problem or achieve a goal.

Debugging: Identifying and removing errors from scripts and programs.

Decomposition: Tackling larger problems by breaking them into smaller parts so that we can explain the process either to someone or to a computer.

Abstraction: The process of removing or reducing details from a complex object to facilitate focus on relevant concepts.

Generalisation: Transferring a problem-solving process to a wide range of problems.

Procedure: Block of code that performs a specific task.

Variable: A value, which can change depending on conditions. Variables are used for holding on to a value to use later.

Loop: A sequence of instructions that are repeated until a specific task achieved.

Pseudocode: Pseudocode can be defined as a 'text-based' algorithmic design tool – basically, a simple way of writing programming code in English.

Conditional: An instruction in a program that is only executed when a specific condition met.

Need to know: essential subject knowledge for teachers and pupils

What is Boolean logic?

Boolean logic is named after the 19th-century mathematician George Boole. It is a type of data with two values: 'true' or 'false'. In a binary number system, each bit has a value of '1' or '0', therefore Boolean logic fits well into computer science. You start with a coding statement that can be either true or false. Boolean logic uses AND, OR, NOT and related operators to evaluate whether your statement is TRUE or FALSE.

Operator	Evaluation
AND	True only if both conditions are true.
OR	True if either condition is true.
NOT	True if the condition is false.

Computer programs make use of Boolean logic all the time. Let's say you are trying to log on to your email account, the computer will check that you have entered the correct user name AND password before it allows you to sign into your account. If either one of these conditions is false, you will not be able to log on to your email account. Using Boolean algebra on two or more conditions can allow us to make our program shorter, which will mean it takes less time to run and makes our code much easier to read. Booleans can also be seen as functions that are the answer to yes or no questions and can be used to perform tests. For example, using a Boolean to indicate if the temperature is above or below room temperature.

Boolean logic is frequently used when searching a database; because the Internet is a huge computer database, searching is based on the logical relationship among search terms, referred to as the 'principles of Boolean logic'.

List of websites to practise Boolean logic:

www.neuroproductions.be/logic-lab/

www.bbc.co.uk/cbbc/games/doctor-who-game

www.bbc.co.uk/schools/0/computing/29831477

www.advanced-ict.info/interactive/boolean.html

www.kidzsearch.com/boolify/

Unplugged Activity 1: Space Race

Overview

This is a multiplayer board game that is played in 'draw five, play one' format. The game aims to help students to practise determining the outcome of conditionals and evaluate logical statements to decide which instructions to follow through programming their characters to reach pre-set targets. You need to download the 'Space Race' game kit from **www.ictinpractice.com/space-race-2/**

Computational thinking features developed

Logic, algorithms, evaluation, tinkering, conditional

Cross-curricular links

Science

Learning about the planets and their position in space. You could also set targets involving specific characteristics of the planets rather than their images, e.g. the target is the planet that is closest to the Earth.

Mathematics

Targets can be set using the coordinates, which would help students to practise reading coordinates. By using different angle values for turning left and right, they can also learn about types of angles and directional language, e.g. turn left 45 degrees.

Age range

This activity can be used both in Key Stage 1 and Key Stage 2 with modification. Tasks and program cards can be redesigned to create more complex algorithms.

Lesson plan

Learning objectives

- To predict what will happen for a sequence of instructions.
- To use programming commands to create a sequence to achieve a specific outcome (algorithms).
- To use repeat commands.
- To practise determining the outcome of conditionals.

Key words and questions

Algorithms – an algorithm is a set of precise instructions to solve a problem or achieve a goal.

Logic – logical reasoning is used to reason and explain the behaviour of programs. In other words, to explain why something happens.

Conditionals – an instruction in a program that is only executed when a specific condition is met.

Evaluation – evaluation takes place in our daily lives all the time. In computer science, evaluation refers to checking how appropriate solutions are for the purpose they are intended.

Tinkering – trying things out and improving upon ideas through trial and error.

- How do algorithms work?
- Can you describe the most efficient route to travel from home to school?

Activities

Time	Teacher activity	Student activity	Resources
10 mins	The teacher asks the children to think about the most efficient way of travelling – needs extra 1 to school from home. How did they create this solution?	Children to discuss the most efficient route to travel from home to school. Children to explore the game pack and ask questions to clarify issues in advance.	Space Race board game resources (available at: **www. ictinpractice.com/ space-race-2/**).
35 mins	The teacher will introduce the game to the children and discuss the vocabulary at the beginning of the lesson. The rules must be read out and any misconceptions should be dealt with before the game commences.	Students play the 'Space Race' game in groups and keep a record of any problems that they might have come across or make suggestions to improve the game either on paper or using an audio/video recording device.	
15 mins	At the end of the activity, the teacher will hold a discussion session for the children to share their ideas about how they created a sequence of code using programming commands to reach their targets. Teachers should encourage students to talk about their problem-solving activities through purposeful questioning.	They should discuss their findings at the end of the session focusing on how they designed the most efficient route for their set location on the game board.	

Success criteria and assessment

Peer assessment would work well with this activity. You could pair children to evaluate their activities during the game. Players can check if their opponents were able to create algorithms for their character to travel to the target planet. They could also share how they designed the most efficient route using their programming commands at the end of the game.

Scope for differentiation and extension

This game can be modified to meet the diverse needs of learners. More complex instructions such as turn left 45 degrees can be used to challenge children who are ready to move on. Rather than showing the picture of the target planet, children can be read the characteristics of their target planet, which will help them to use their knowledge to determine their target planet. Those who found it hard to create a sequence to achieve a task can work as a partner to support each other.

Unplugged Activity 2: Can you find the criminal?

Overview

It is important for the teachers to introduce how to evaluate statements through hands-on activities. The session should start with a '10 questions' game for children to practise determining the outcome of conditionals using Boolean logic.

They should then be given an opportunity to apply Boolean logic through solving puzzles based on detective stories. This session can be taught as a combination of literacy and computing sessions. Although we have provided an example crime scene for students to use in this session, you could spend a lesson where your students can create their own crime scenes in groups and then exchange them with other groups to solve them.

Computational thinking features developed

Conditional, If–then-else statement, Function

Cross-curricular links

Science, History, Geography
The '10 questions' activity could be created using statements related to any topic in Science, History and Geography. For example, learners could classify animals by evaluating statements about them.

Literacy
Although we have provided a simple detective story in this activity to be used to teach about how Boolean logic works, students can be asked to create their own puzzle stories in literacy lessons for their peers.

Age range

This activity can be used in Key Stage 2 with children aged 9 and above.

Lesson plan

Learning objectives

Use logical reasoning to determine the outcome of conditionals.

Evaluate statements to decide which part of a program to follow.

Key words and questions

Conditional – a statement that can be true or false depending on the conditions.

If–then–else statement – uses a Boolean expression to determine which one of two statements to execute.

Function: A sequence of codes that can be called again and again.

● How can you use Boolean logic to search about detective stories on the Internet?

Activities

Time	Teacher activity	Student activity	Resources
20 mins	● **Starter activity** ● **Lesson sequence for '10 Questions' activity** ● Display the 10 Questions card (Table 7.1) on a board and ask children to answer it. ● Select a student to lead the activity. ● Put all the students' cards into a box and ask one of them to choose one. ● Give the selected card to the student who will lead the activity. ● The student who is responsible for managing the activity asks a question, e.g. have you got brown eyes? Is your favourite food chocolate? ● The students all stand up and then sit down only if their answer to the questions is FALSE. ● Make sure that the students know how to ask questions using 'OR' and 'AND'. ● Play this game a few times until the children develop an awareness of Boolean logic. ● You can add more questions to make it more challenging.	Children to play the '10 Questions' game. Pupils to come up with their own questions to make the game more challenging.	Deck of cards. How to code with cards sheet. Pen and paper.
30 mins	● **Main activity** ● **Who stole my game console?** ● This activity is inspired by the Boole2Schools project designed by University College Cork. You can find more puzzles and activities for children to learn about Boolean principles on their website **http://georgeboole.com/boole2school/**	Children to work in groups to solve the crime case and record their solutions on the problem-solving sheet (Figure 7.1).	

Time	Teacher activity	Student activity	Resources
	• Display the 'Who stole my game console?' story on the board and ask the children to discuss in groups how they would solve this problem.		
10 mins	• Teachers to ask the children to share their solutions and discuss their methods.	Children can explain their solutions to either the whole class or another group and compare their strategies that helped them to solve the crime case.	

Success criteria and assessment

Children's problem-solving sheets would allow us to see how they had worked out their solution, which in turn would help us to understand the strategies that they had used. It is important that the teacher does not let the children delete their workings out. Another criteria could be whether or not the children can apply Boolean logic principles to create their own puzzle problems for their friends to solve. This also can show us if they understood how Boolean logic works.

Scope for differentiation and extension

'10 Questions' session is an introduction activity. To extend or challenge students, the number of questions could be increased with the use of 'and', 'or', 'not' terms.

The puzzle problems can be created with different levels of difficulties to meet the needs of all the students. Asking children to create their own crime scene would support them with applying their understanding of how Boolean logic works.

Table 7.1   10 Questions card

ALL ABOUT ME!	ANSWERS
1. What is your hair colour?	1.
2. What month were you born?	2.
3. What is your favourite colour?	3.
4. What is your favourite food?	4.
5. Do you like playing computer games?	5.
6. Do you have a pet?	6.
7. Do you have any siblings?	7.
8. What is your favourite sport?	8.
9. Who is your favourite singer?	9.
10. Do you speak more than one language?	10.

Main activity sheet

Solving a crime case

Who stole my games console?

Yesterday I returned from a week's holiday from Australia. When I arrived home, the door was open and everything was thrown around. Strangely, my TV, my laptop and all of the valuable items were not stolen. I was surprised, 'if they were thieves surely they would steal everything,' I thought to myself. I called the police directly. We went through all the items in the house. It was unbelievable that they only stole my game console and my games. The police officers were amazing and they quickly arrested four people with a known history of crimes in my area. But it was so hard to find out who the criminal was. They all made statements. Can you read their statements below and help us to find who stole my games console and games? Remember, each one of them told one lie.

George

It wasn't Niki,

It was Megan

Megan

It wasn't Jack,

It wasn't Niki

Niki

It was Jack,

It was Megan

Jack

It was Niki,

It wasn't George

MY SOLUTION

Figure 7.1 Problem-solving sheet

Unplugged Activity 3: Coding with cards
Overview

This activity starts with a whole class activity for the children to practise using and applying conditionals through a simple game. They learn to set and follow conditionals so that they can become confident at using 'if' and 'else' statements.

They then move on to playing a card game, where they can learn that we call 'if statements' conditionals because there is a condition linked to them. If the statement is 'true', then we carry out the instruction inside the 'if statement'. If it is not true then

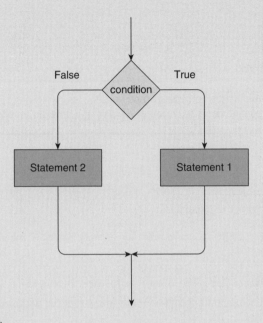

Figure 7.2 Conditionals

we execute the program inside the 'else'. Explain that this is how computers make decisions. It is good to use Figure 7.2 to explain conditionals.

Computational thinking features developed

Logic, Conditionals, Evaluation

Cross-curricular links

Science, History and Geography
The starter activity can be introduced during Science, History and Geography sessions as the questions can be linked to various topics, e.g. Materials, Romans, Habitats.

Mathematics
Mathematical principles could be used to create conditions for the card game. For example, 'if the number ≤ 7 then miss a turn, else receive 2 points'.

Age range

This activity can be used both in Key Stage 1 and Key Stage 2 with modification. 'If statements' and 'else statements' could be redesigned to create conditionals with different range of difficulties.

Lesson plan

Learning objectives

- To practise determining the outcome of conditionals.
- To evaluate logical statements to decide which part of a program to follow.

Key words and questions

Logic – logical reasoning is used to reason and explain the behaviour of programs. In other words, to explain why something happens.

Conditionals – an instruction in a program that is only executed when a specific condition is met.

Evaluation – evaluation takes place in our daily lives all the time. In computer science, evaluation refers to checking how appropriate solutions are for the purpose they are intended.

- What is a conditional statement? Can you give an example?

- How do computers make decisions?

Activities

Time	Teacher activity	Student activity	Resources
20 mins	The teacher will introduce the activity to the children and discuss the vocabulary at the beginning of the lesson. The statements could be based on any specific topics that the children are learning about in other curriculum subjects. After they have demonstrated the activity, they could ask them to come up with their own statement. Make sure that this activity is carried out in a large space. Give the children a condition such as: If I show you a card with a number higher than 10 sit down, or else touch your nose. If I say an odd number turn around, or else jump up. If I draw a rhombus clap your hands, or else shake your head. Or you could make statements about the Romans and explain to the children that if the statement is true they need to swirl around, if it is wrong they need to do a little dance. For example: • The Romans invaded Britain because they were looking for chocolate. • The Romans called London 'Londinium'. • The Romans gave us central heating.	Children to follow the conditionals that are given by their teachers. Pupils to come up with their own conditionals for the selected topic.	Deck of cards.

Time	Teacher activity	Student activity	Resources
30 mins	**Main activity** Tell the children that they will be playing a card game in groups using standard playing card decks. The only difference is that they will have conditions written for the cards to follow. See the 'How to code with cards' sheet for the rules. Demonstrate how to play the game with a few children and provide each child with a 'How to code with cards' sheet. Let the children play the game in groups of 4-5. They must have paper and a pen to keep the points tally for each player.	Children to play 'coding with cards' game in groups. They could write their own conditionals for using the Jacks, Queens and Kings on the empty cards.	'How to code with cards' sheet. Pen and paper.

Success criteria and assessment

Provide the children with a medium to keep a record of their learning journey in computing. This could be a blog or a wiki. The reason for this is that if the children are working collaboratively, it is very difficult to assess their learning. If we provide opportunities for them to reflect on their problem-solving activities, we might gain an understanding of their learning process, which would help us to assess their attainment. The children could also use their blog to collect badges for the skills that they have developed.

Scope for differentiation and extension

This game can be modified to meet the diverse needs of learners. Rather than using *pseudocode*, you could use Python or Java to write the conditions for each card. This would allow them to practise textual code through a physical game. For those who are not confident, the conditions can be kept simple without the 'AND' term.

Discussion

Key concept: algorithms are all around us

An algorithm is a set of precise instructions to solve a problem or achieve a goal. Algorithms are at the core of computer science. Computer scientists design algorithms to solve problems in their programs. We use algorithms to design solutions to complete our daily tasks all the time. For example, when we travel from one place to another, we look for the most efficient route either manually or using applications such as the Transport For London journey planner on the Internet. There are many algorithms that will help us to accomplish the same task, so the focus is to find the fastest or shortest route.

Creating algorithms involves selecting instructions and then putting them into a sequence to complete a task or create a rule. We can use repetition to make our instructions shorter or more flexible. We use algorithms in mathematics when solving problems, in science when designing an experiment, in literacy when planning our writing task.

In **Early Years,** daily activities create opportunities for the sequencing element of algorithms. Children line up to go to lunch; they take turns in using a computer or other equipment. They retell the stories that they have read either at home or in the classrooms. They talk about how they get dressed.

In **Key Stage 1,** pupils need to know what algorithms are and how they are used in programs. It is important to start with hands-on activities.

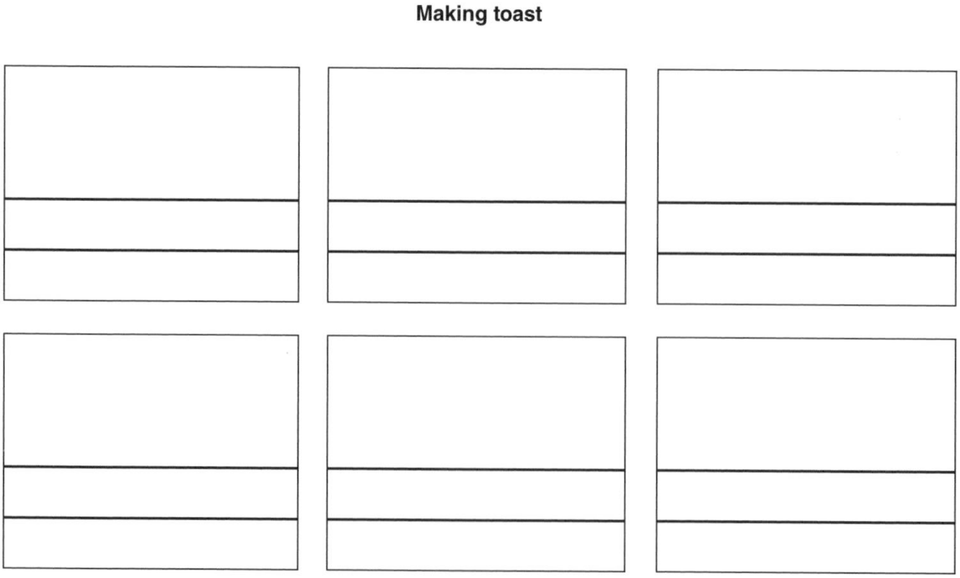

Making toast

Figure 7.3   Making toast

- They can design a dance routine.

- They can create a storyboard for making toast (see Figure 7.3), or cleaning their teeth.

- They can use floor robots to implement their algorithms such as retelling the events of a story or moving around a maze and compare this with the algorithms that they implemented on an on-screen program, e.g. LOGO. They can even use human robots to test their algorithms.

In **Key Stage 2,** pupils are expected to design programs for a specific purpose. They start with designing their algorithm for their program. This can be in a format of a storyboard or pseudocode or a combination of both. They use logical reasoning to explain how simple algorithms work. They explain why they designed their algorithm in the way that they did and how their algorithm achieves the expected outcome. They also use logical reasoning to identify errors in their algorithms and debug them. They understand that computers need precise instructions to accomplish tasks.

Reflective questions

- How does Boolean logic work?

- What is a conditional statement?

- How is Boolean logic used in search engines?

- What is an algorithm and how does it work?

- How can we teach the main elements of algorithms: sequencing, selection and repetition using real-life examples?

Summary and Key Points

This book provides a range of activities to help pupils develop their computational thinking skills through board and card games. The focus of this chapter has been on that of Boolean logic and conditionals. Boolean logic uses AND, OR, NOT and related operators to evaluate whether a statement is TRUE or FALSE. In the 'Can you find the criminal?' activity, children use Boolean logic to solve puzzle-based detective stories. This is an important skill to learn as this is how computers make decisions.

Through playing board and card games children develop their skills to design algorithms to achieve a specific goal. In 'Space Race', the children had to design the most efficient route to travel to their set destination, which involves using sequencing and repetition elements of designing algorithms.

A progression in conditionals from EYFS to Key Stage 2 has been provided which includes ideas on what progression in algorithms is like through the primary phase and includes ideas for developing it.

Resources and further reading

The Barefoot Project **www.barefootcas.org.uk**
A Department for Education project created to demystify computational thinking for primary teachers.
Includes teach yourself concept resources, and exemplar classroom activities.

BBC Bitesize Algorithms **www.bbc.co.uk/guides/z3whpv4**
An overview of what algorithms are, aimed at primary pupils. It is a useful resource for teachers.

The George Boole project by University College Cork **http://georgeboole.com/boole2school/**
Provided information about George Boole and has activity ideas to teach Boolean logic.

Quickstart Primary Handbook **www.quickstartcomputing.org**
A Department for Education and Microsoft project helping teachers deliver CPD for primary and
secondary computing.

References

Department for Education (DfE) (2011) *Teachers' Standards*. Available from **www.gov.uk/government/
uploads/system/uploads/attachment_data/file/283566/Teachers_standard_information.pdf**
(accessed 23 December 2015).

Department for Education (2013) *Computing Programmes of Study: Key Stages: 1 and 2*. Available from
**www.gov.uk/government/uploads/system/uploads/attachment_data/file/239033/PRIMARY_
national_curriculum_-_Computing.pdf**

Dewey, J (1938) *Experience and Education*. New York: Simon & Schuster.

Piaget, J (1954) *The Construction of Reality in the Child*. New York: Ballantine.

Piaget, J (1970) *Logic and Psychology*. New York: Basic Books.

Piaget, J and Inhelder, B (1969) *The Psychology of the Child*. New York: Basic Books,

Vygotsky, S (1978) Interaction between learning and development. *Mind in Society,* 79–91.
Available from **www.psy.cmu.edu/~siegler/vygotsky78.pdf**

Chapter 8
C**O**KS

In order that the duties of the Cook may be properly performed, and that he may be able to reproduce esteemed dishes with certainty, all terms of indecision should be banished from his art. Accordingly, what is known only to him, will, in these pages, be made known to others. In them all those indecisive terms expressed by a bit of this, some of that, a small piece of that, and a handful of the other, shall never be made use of, but all quantities be precisely and explicitly stated. With a desire, also, that all ignorance on this most essential part of the culinary art should disappear, and that a uniform system of weights and measures should be adopted, we give an account of the weights which answer to certain measures.

Mrs Beeton (Beeton, 1861)

Introduction

Cooking is fun and a great social way to use and learn about computational thinking.

Are you the type of cook who must have a glossy photo and a detailed recipe? Do you abandon a dish because you just can't find that elusive ingredient? Or are you a confident rummager, who peers in the back of the cupboard and knocks up a savoury bake, a tasty omelette, a staple sponge cake? Do you adapt from just two or three template recipes in a well-worn book, or even from memory?

Family recipes are handed down. Basics are taught in primary school cookery classes or online with the latest celebrity chef. Students are sent off to college with that basic recipe book or a link to that good food website.

But at what point do we turn from trembling sous chef to confident creative cook? Perhaps when we have spotted some culinary design patterns and worked out how to abstract and generalise in the kitchen.

This chapter explores recipes, using this familiar context to learn about computational thinking concepts. Here children find out what is most important in a recipe, compare recipes to find similarities and differences, and are creative as they reuse a template to make their own new recipe. We make peppermint creams, fruit salad and perfect pasta or yuk pasta (for trolls) to learn about abstraction and generalisation.

The activities are:

- *wrong recipes – learning about abstraction;*

- *recipe detectives – learning about pattern;*

- *copy and paste pasta – learning about generalisation.*

Links to Teachers' Standards

The following Teachers' Standards are particularly relevant to this chapter:

TS1b Set goals that stretch and challenge pupils.
TS3a Have a secure knowledge of the relevant subject(s) and curriculum areas.
TS4e Contribute to the design and provision of an engaging curriculum.

(DfE, 2011)

Links to the National Curriculum Programmes of Study

The purpose of the study and aims of the primary computing programme state:

A high-quality computing education equips pupils to use computational thinking and creativity to understand and change the world.

The National Curriculum for computing aims to ensure that all pupils:

- can understand and apply the fundamental principles and concepts of computer science, including abstraction, logic, algorithms and data representation;
- can analyse problems in computational terms.

(DfE, 2013)

There are no specific subject content outcomes in the primary computing curriculum that use the terms abstraction, pattern or generalisation. However, these concepts are fundamental elements of computational thinking and without abstraction, pattern and generalisation we could not create algorithms and without algorithms we could not design, write and debug programs.

Abstraction, pattern and generalisation contribute to children's progression across the computing curriculum but particularly in:

Key Stage 1

Pupils should be taught to:

- understand what algorithms are;
- create and debug simple programs.

Key Stage 2

Pupils should be taught to:

- design, write and debug programs.

Unplugged Activity 1: Wrong recipes

Overview

Chapter 1 investigated instructions for bossing robots about and helped us learn about algorithms. Recipes are algorithms. Here we use recipes, culinary algorithms, to find out about abstraction.

Wrong recipes are used to guide children to the conclusion that having the right information is vital. Essential information is missed from some recipes, additional unimportant elements are added to overcomplicate others. Children learn that recipe design is about abstraction, developing their skills to ignore what is unimportant, and to include only what is needed.

As well as reading wrong recipes, children could try them out to see what the impact is of having too much or too little detail. If you do this, you may need to model how to follow the recipe exactly. Our natural instinct is to fill in any gaps or ignore incorrect information.

Wrong recipes could be adapted to be used within any cookery scheme of work. Whether making a salad, pasta or milkshake, you could create some wrong recipes for children to learn about abstraction.

This activity could be part of a guided reading lesson, or it could be a starter or plenary in a non-fiction instruction text writing lesson.

Computational thinking features developed

Algorithmic thinking is when we create precise steps or rules that make something happen or get something done. Here the algorithm is the recipe.

Abstraction is the process of making something *easier* to understand by working out what *is* most important and *must be included* and what is *not* important and can be ignored or hidden. In our examples abstraction happens when we work out what we must include in a recipe for it to work, and what can be left out.

There is no requirement in the programme of study for children to learn to use the word 'abstraction'. A simpler phrase might be:

- include the right detail;
- ignore what we do not need;
- remove the unnecessary detail.

Cross-curricular links

Design and Technology
A context of recipes is used for this activity linking it to the cooking and nutrition component of the Design and Technology programmes of study.

Literacy

When reading recipes, children work to understand non-fiction texts, exploring new vocabulary, text structure and meaning.

Age range

Key Stage 1 and Key Stage 2.

Learning objectives

- I can say what should be included in a recipe.

- I can say what should not be included in a recipe.

Key words and questions

include, important, ignore.

- What must we include? Why is that important? Is that needed? Why? What if we removed that part? What could we do without? Why?

Resources

Prepare 'wrong recipes' before the lesson. These could be aligned to recipes that you have used in previous cookery lessons, or that have a context relevant to your current topic. Here are some examples.

Activity ideas

- Without giving too much away about the objectives of the lesson, ask mixed-ability groups to read the recipe and to say what they think about them and to improve the recipes.

- As a class, discuss the children's ideas, asking children to explain their reasoning.

- Draw out the idea that in some examples there is unnecessary detail that can be removed, and in others insufficient detail that needs to be added.

- Start to develop a class 'success criteria' for an 'ideal recipe'.

- Model how to create two versions of a recipe, one with lots of 'wrong' features and one that is more ideal.

- Ask groups to create their two alternate versions, perhaps with at least one example of too much detail and one example of not enough detail.

- Groups can then present their versions explaining their recipe designs. Or groups might peer assess other teams' designs, identifying which they think are the 'too much/not enough details' versions. This may provoke some hot debate!

How to make Peppermint Creams		Making Fruit Salad
Ingredients	**Equipment**	**You will need**
Some sugar	A big bowl	2 apples each weighing 27g exactly
Some peppermint extract	A spoon	1 banana of length 26cm
Large sheets of white paper	Scissors	24 green grapes of length 1.5cm and weighing 1g
140 tiny golden stars	Gold pen	
	Green felt tip	A chopping board
	Ruby red felt tip	A sharp knife
		A bowl

Instructions (Peppermint Creams)

1. Put the sugar in the bowl
2. Add the peppermint extract
3. Mix it up
4. Make the paper cases by drawing 35 circles, each 10 cm wide on the paper. Cut each circle out carefully with sharp scissors. These are your cases. Decorate each case with 4 tiny golden stars. Draw three gold and green Dragons on each case, add tiny ruby eyes and red flames cascading out of their wide open jaws. Ensure that the one wing is green and one is golden
5. Put the mixture in the cases.

What you do (Fruit Salad)

1. Peel the apples and chop them up.
2. Peel the banana and chop it up.
3. Put the apple, banana and grapes in the bowl.
4. Eat and enjoy.

Figure 8.1 Example recipes

Success criteria and assessment

Children have met their learning outcome if they can identify one or two 'too much detail' and 'not enough detail' elements of a recipe and explain their reasoning. If you do not have evidence of this from the main tasks, ask children to rewrite a step in a recipe that is either with too much detail, or missing detail. This could be done using mini whiteboards, scribed by an adult, or recorded using a digital device.

Scope for differentiation and extension

Younger children, or those requiring more support, particularly in literacy, may need to work in groups or work with an adult. Adapt the complexity of the vocabulary to your class.

Take this further by discussing problem-solving techniques in general.

Lead a class discussion on how the ability to work out what is most important to include and the ability to ignore (or hide) information that we do not need are very important skills. Perhaps link this to solving maths word problems and comprehension activities.

You can also link this to planning in other subjects. When we plan we only think of the main parts we need to deal with. We sketch out a summary of what we intend to do. We do not worry about the detail. For example, when planning a non-fiction text we summarise the characters, setting and outline a plot. If planning a DT project we might include the audience, purpose, materials we plan to use, equipment and the main steps.

Once children have thought about what should be included in a recipe, they could then follow recipes and see what happens for themselves. In doing this they will start to look more closely at algorithm design.

Phil Bagge's famous Sandwich Bot showcases how children can learn about sequencing and precision in food-based algorithms. Watch the hilarious video on YouTube as Phil's pupils programme him to make a jam sandwich: **www.youtube.com/watch?v=leBEFaVHllE**

Linking to the real world and computing

There are further opportunities here to link the concept of abstraction directly to real-world scenarios as well as to programming projects that pupils may do themselves.

Real world
In 1931, Henry Charles Beck created a very famous abstraction, the London Underground Map. People were finding it difficult to navigate the underground because the maps showed a lot of detail of where the train lines went. His map ignored the physical distances between stations, the exact direction of each track, and the landmarks above ground. He focused on what was needed for the task in hand, showing just the stations and colour-coded lines.

Computing
Being able to abstract is a fundamental skill required when developing computer systems. A flight simulator is not a real aeroplane; it cannot fly you from New York to London, but it has the right detail to be able to train a pilot so that they can learn to fly this route safely. An online dating app does not have tiny people sitting inside our phones waiting to be asked a question about their favourite food; a designer has chosen what data should be held to represent each person and the app has an abstraction of each possible date.

Programming projects
Suppose we are going to create a simple simulation of the solar system. First, we ask 'What are the most important aspects that we want to include?' We might say that the Earth moving around the Sun is essential but that we can ignore the speed, distances, sizes involved. By being able to focus on the most important aspects, we simplify and make a problem easier to tackle. See the Barefoot activity Solar System Simulation for more ideas in this area, available from **www.barefootcas.org.uk**

Unplugged Activity 2: Recipe detectives

Overview

In earlier chapters you have already learned about the power of pattern, how comparing two or more things helps us understand something in more detail. In this activity we are detectives as we compare recipes to discover common aspects. By doing this we learn about pattern and then generalisation.

Where possible use real-world recipes as examples; however, you may find there are few commercial recipes with the features you want to exemplify. Writing your own simple versions may be required to start with, but as children write their own, keep them, reuse them and share with other teachers.

There are two phases to this activity:

1. Spot what is the same and what is different across different versions of a recipe, e.g. compare the recipes for making an autumn fruit salad and an exotic fruit salad.

2. Make a template for a general version of the recipe, e.g. make a general fruit salad recipe.

This activity can be undertaken as a paper exercise, but it is much more fun, more memorable and effective if children actually follow recipes and see what happens for themselves.

However, care will be needed to ensure that children are still attending to the objective of the activity – to look for similarities and differences. You could introduce key reflection points to stop pupils and compare their progress, or record progress so that you can reflect on mid points and motivate groups by awarding points to teams if they spot similarities/differences between recipes.

This activity could be adapted to be used within any cookery scheme of work, whether making a salad, pasta or milkshake, create different versions of a recipe for children to learn about pattern and generalisation.

Computational thinking features developed

Pattern is spotting similarities and differences. We use pattern when comparing recipes to see what common ingredients, equipment, steps, pictures and layouts are used to make dishes such as peppermint creams, fruit salad or pasta. Here we are recipe detectives as we play spot the instructions' difference.

Generalisation is using the patterns we have spotted to solve a new problem. Here common features of recipes are used to create a template recipe that could be reused and adapted, applying the template, the generalisation.

There is no Requirement in the programme of study for children to learn to use the word 'generalisation'. A simpler translation might be used such as:

- find the common parts;
- make a template;
- create blocks you can reuse.

In some computational thinking frameworks *pattern* is included as a component or synonym for generalisation, rather than as a separate concept.

In some computational thinking frameworks a concept of evaluation is included:

> *Evaluation is the process of ensuring that a solution, whether an algorithm, system or process is a good one that it is fit for purpose.*

> (Csizmadia *et al.*, 2015)

When we generalise we decide what to include in our template and we evaluate the choices that we have.

Cross-curricular links

Design and Technology
A context of recipes is used for this activity linking it to the cooking and nutrition component of the Design and Technology programmes of study.

Literacy
When reading recipes children work to understand non-fiction texts, exploring new vocabulary, text structure and meaning.

Age range

Key Stage 1 and Key Stage 2.

Lesson plan

Learning objectives

- I can say what is the same and different.
- I can suggest what to include in a template recipe.

Key words and questions

same, different, template, reuse, general, generic

- What is the same? Why is it different? Which is the best? Why? What can we reuse? What must we have in the template? Why? Could we remove that from the template? Why/why not?

Resources

Find or prepare 'different versions' of a recipe before the lesson. Here are some examples. There are further examples in the Barefoot resources 'Reusing Recipes' available at **www.barefootcas.org**

Activity ideas

For the theme of *Pattern*:

- Provide groups with different versions of a recipe and ask them to spot what is the same and what is different across them. Children could highlight things that are the same.

- Different groups could use recipes and then compare their experiences too – but this would fall within extra lessons.

- As a class, discuss what the children have found is the same/different across the recipes.

OJ Fruit Salad	Going Bananas
You will need	**Ingredients**
1 apple	3 bananas
1 banana	1 apple
1 orange	A handful of grapes
A handful of grapes	A squeeze of lemon juice
A chopping board	
A sharp knife	**Equipment**
A bowl	A chopping board
A lemon squeezer	A sharp knife
	A bowl
What you do	**Instructions**
1. Peel the apple and chop it up.	1. Peel the bananas
2. Peel the banana and chop it up.	2. Chop them up.
3. Cut the orange in half and squeeze it.	3. Put in bowl.
4. Put the apple, banana and grapes in the bowl and cover with the orange juice.	4. Peel the apple
5. Eat and enjoy.	5. Chop it up.
	6. Put in bowl.
	7. Wash grapes
	8. Put in the bowl.
	9. Pour the lemon juice over the fruit.

(Continued)

Figure 8.2 (Continued)

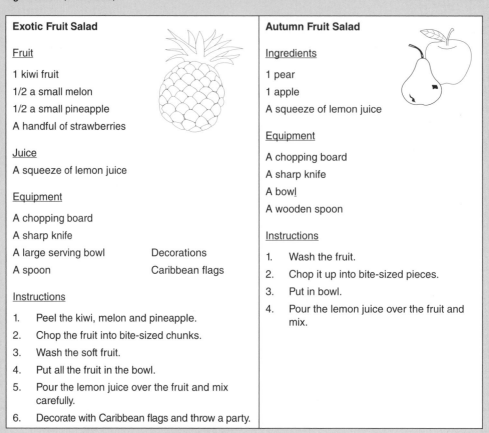

Exotic Fruit Salad

Fruit

1 kiwi fruit
1/2 a small melon
1/2 a small pineapple
A handful of strawberries

Juice
A squeeze of lemon juice

Equipment

A chopping board
A sharp knife
A large serving bowl   Decorations
A spoon   Caribbean flags

Instructions

1. Peel the kiwi, melon and pineapple.
2. Chop the fruit into bite-sized chunks.
3. Wash the soft fruit.
4. Put all the fruit in the bowl.
5. Pour the lemon juice over the fruit and mix carefully.
6. Decorate with Caribbean flags and throw a party.

Autumn Fruit Salad

Ingredients

1 pear
1 apple
A squeeze of lemon juice

Equipment

A chopping board
A sharp knife
A bowl
A wooden spoon

Instructions

1. Wash the fruit.
2. Chop it up into bite-sized pieces.
3. Put in bowl.
4. Pour the lemon juice over the fruit and mix.

Figure 8.2 Different versions of a recipe

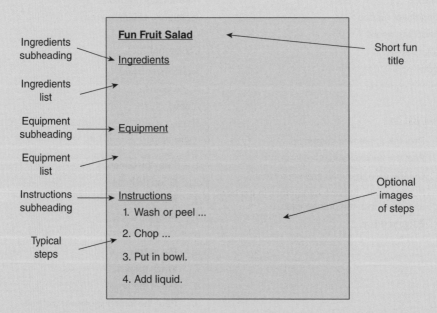

Figure 8.3 A generalised fruit salad recipe

For the theme of *Generalisation*:

- Guide the discussion to deciding on what parts might be good for a template of a general fruit salad recipe.

- Groups could cut up their recipes to find the common parts and then prioritise which parts they must have.

- Perhaps use a labelled diagram or mind map to capture the main features of the recipes. Children may come up with new features that they think are important.

Success criteria and assessment

Children have met the pattern learning outcome if they can identify one or two similarities and differences across recipes. They have met the generalisation outcome if they can suggest something that could be included in a template recipe.

If you do not have evidence of this from the main tasks, ask children to improve a recipe, and to explain how theirs is the same or different.

Scope for differentiation and extension

Younger children, or those requiring more support, particularly in literacy, may need to work in groups or work with an adult. Adapt the complexity of the vocabulary to your class.

Groups could look at recipes for other food types, e.g. making savoury salads, baking cakes, preparing milkshakes looking for pattern and generalisation more widely across recipes.

This activity could be adapted to be used within any cookery scheme of work. Whether making a salad, pasta or milkshake, create some wrong recipes for children to learn about abstraction.

This activity could be part of a guided reading lesson, or a comprehension starter or plenary.

Linking to the real world and computing

There are further opportunities here to link the concept of generalisation directly to real-world scenarios as well as to programming projects that pupils may do themselves.

Real world

Spotting what is the same and what is different are problem-solving skills that we use everyday. As we wake up in the morning and notice it is colder than yesterday, we are comparing our expectations to reality.

Computing

Often in the development of solutions, looking for patterns is a stepping stone to finding something to reuse or creating something that can be used in more than one place. This saves time and money! For example, if developing software for an online shop, the developers might look for other systems that already do similar things and see how they can reuse or adapt these products. Reuse might come in many guises from reusing a block of code, adapting user interface guidelines, adopting industry guidelines for payment security, to modifying an 'off-the-shelf' package for the whole thing.

Programming projects

Suppose children are going to create a game in Scratch. We might ask them to start by looking at several games and compare them. We might list common features or differences. We might then decide what the common features of games are and create a list or template of what is needed. When we do this we are generalising. We may find graphics, instructions, code and other features in the games we reviewed that we can reuse. At the same time we are also using the skill of abstracting as we decide what is most important to include.

See the Barefoot activity 'Make a Game' for more ideas in this area: **http://barefootcas. org.uk/programme-of-study/design-programs-accomplish-specific-goals/ ks2-make-a-game-project-design-write-and-debug-programs/**

Unplugged Activity 3: Copy and paste pasta

Overview

The activity can be undertaken as a stand-alone lesson or it can follow on from Activity 2.

Here we further explore generalisation, using a template to create a new version of something. You could use the template created from Activity 2 or create a new template. In this activity we create a new template for pasta and then children use it to make a new dish for themselves or for a fantasy character.

Children reuse components, seeing how they can quickly design a new meal without having to worry about the detail of the parts they are reusing.

Computational thinking features developed

Generalisation is using the patterns we have spotted to solve a new problem. Here common features of recipes are used to create a template recipe that can then be reused and adapted, applying the template: the generalisation. Shared writing gives children the chance to help make the template pasta recipe. They then get creative as they adapt it for a new pasta meal.

There is no requirement in the programme of study for children to learn to use the word 'generalisation'. A simpler translation might be used such as:

- find the common parts;
- make a template;
- create blocks you can reuse.

Design patterns are commonly occurring templates or approaches that can be reused in lots of different situations. Having a design pattern can save lots of time and money, it is the idea of not reinventing the wheel, just adapting a generic wheel design to what is needed for the task in hand.

In cookery there are many design patterns that we reuse. For example, the same basic ingredients and methods are used whether making dough for pizza, small sweet rolls, or hearty savoury loaves. The ubiquitous sponge cake recipe can be repurposed with different frostings, baked in different shapes and sizes to create one or two simple butterfly buns, or a magnificent chocolate dinosaur birthday cake.

Cross-curricular links

Design and Technology
A context of recipes is used for this activity linking it to the cooking and nutrition component of the Design and Technology programmes of study.

Literacy
When reading recipes children work to understand non-fiction texts, exploring new vocabulary, text structure and meaning.

Age range

Key Stage 1 and Key Stage 2.

Lesson plan

Learning objectives

- I can use a template recipe to create a new version of the recipe.
- I can create a template from a group of example recipes.
- I know what a template is for and why it is useful.

Key words and questions

template, reuse, repurpose, change, adapt

- What can we reuse?
- How can we change this?
- What have you changed? Why?
- Why is a template useful?

Resources

Example: real-world pasta recipes
A template pasta recipe.

<Title of pasta dish>	Basic tomato sauce	
Ingredients	Ingredients	
<type of pasta>	1 onion	1 tablespoon of tomato paste
Basic tomato sauce	1 clove of garlic	1/2 teaspoon of sugar
<extra ingredients>	1 tin of tomatoes	Handful of chopped basil
<garnish>	Grind of salt	
	Grind of pepper	
Equipment		
Large pan	Equipment	
Sharp knife	Frying pan	
Chopping board	Sharp knife	
Serving plate	Chopping board	
Spoon	Serving plate	
	Spoon	
Instructions		
1. Using a large pan of water, cook the pasta until cooked. (Follow the instructions on the packet.)	Instructions	
2. Prepare the <extra ingredients> for the pasta sauce.	1. Peel and chop the onion.	
3. Make the tomato sauce.	2. Peel and crush the garlic.	
4. Add <the extra ingredients>	3. Fry the garlic and onion over a medium heat until soft and golden brown.	
5. Combine the pasta and sauce and mix thoroughly.	4. Add the tomatoes, tomato paste and sugar and cook for 10 minutes, stirring occasionally to make sure it does not stick to the pan.	
6. Add the <garnish>	5. Add salt and pepper to taste.	
7. Eat and enjoy.	6. Add the basil and stir thoroughly.	

Figure 8.4 Pasta recipe and template

Activity ideas

- Either as a whole class or in groups, read a selection of pasta recipes. Discuss what common aspects there are in the recipes.

- Lead a guided writing session to create a general pasta dish template. See the resource example above.

- Discuss how you could replace the tomato sauce ingredient with a more detailed separate recipe, or how you might have a separate recipe to make the pasta from scratch.

- Model how to use the general template to create your own pasta dish.

  Children use the template to create a new pasta dish independently or in groups. They could do this for themselves or for a fantasy character, e.g. Troll Tagliatelle, Super Mario Spaghetti, Cinderella Shells.

You could photocopy the template (Figure 8.4) and have children fill in the gaps or change other parts as needed.

- You might update the template itself if many groups find they make the same change.

- Children could go on to make their new dishes and test out their culinary algorithm! As they find and fix problems both in the original template and their adaption of it they are practising the skill of debugging.

Success criteria and assessment

Children have met their learning outcomes if they can use a generalisation to create something new, such as create a new template, and if they can explain that they are reusing a template to help save them time.

Scope for differentiation and extension

Younger children, or those requiring more support, particularly in literacy, may need to work in groups or work with an adult. You can adapt the complexity of the vocabulary to your class.

Lead a class discussion on examples of other templates children use, e.g. common sentence structures, approaches for working out spellings, planning formats used in science.

Discuss how templates are used in computing and how parts of a problem can be separated out for reuse, as with the basic tomato sauce. Developers create blocks of code that can be used in lots of different systems. For example, the functionality to detect swipe movements on a mobile phone does not have to be rewritten by every team who create a phone app; there are pre-made blocks of code that can be reused and adapted. Blocks of code that are developed for reuse can be called functions or procedures.

Linking to the real world and computing

There are further opportunities here to link the concept of generalisation directly to real-world scenarios as well as to programming projects that pupils may do themselves.

Real world
Standard sizes, standard fittings, modular designs, guidelines and templates are terms we use when describing many objects, processes and systems in our 'modern' world. For example, imagine the difficulties we would have if every plug on each appliance in your house was different, each perhaps requiring a different voltage, or if builders could install electrical wall sockets of any size and shape.

Computing
Often in the development of solutions, looking for patterns is a stepping stone to finding something to reuse or creating something that can be used in more than one place.

This saves time and money! For example, if developing software for an online shop, the developers might look for other systems that already do similar things and see how they can reuse or adapt these products. Reuse might come in many guises from reusing a block of code, adapting user interface guidelines, adopting industry guidelines for payment security, to modifying an 'off-the-shelf' package for the whole thing.

You might hear about software design patterns. These are reusable solutions for common problems; they are templates that can be adapted by developers for different scenarios.

Programming projects

Suppose we are going to create a quiz. We could look at quizzes, make a list of similarities and differences (pattern), work out the most important aspects (abstraction), and create a template for quizzes (generalisation). Our template might include guidelines, snippets of useful code and examples such as guidelines on creating a quiz master, information on question types and example code, a design for a timer, or a working program with a score that can be adapted.

See the Barefoot activity 'Make a Game' for more ideas in this area available at: **www. barefootcas.org**

Discussion

In our discussion we will consider how the terms 'abstraction' and 'generalisation' are interpreted within computer science teaching, and how researchers are working towards a definition of learning progression at the primary school level.

A little bit of history

Whenever someone writes about computational thinking (CT), Jeanette Wing is often quoted. A Professor of Computer Science at Carnegie Mellon University, and now working for Microsoft, she places abstraction at the heart of computational thinking.

> *The abstraction process – deciding what details we need to highlight and what details we can ignore – underlies computational thinking.*

> (Wing, 2008)

Wing's assertion of the importance of abstraction to computer science and computational thinking seems to be gaining consensus, as national curricula, academic research papers, subject association documents and assessment frameworks include abstraction as a fundamental concept.

The 2013 English National Curriculum for computing aims to ensure that all pupils: *can understand and apply the fundamental principles and concepts of computer science, including abstraction, logic, algorithms and data representation* (DFE, 2013).

Grover & Pea's review of computational thinking includes abstraction and pattern generalisation as an element *now widely accepting as comprising {computational thinking}.* (Grover & Pea, 2013a, p39)

The US College Board's AP Computer Science Principles Curriculum Framework for 2016–17 defines 'abstracting' as one of its computational thinking practices and 'abstraction' as one of its 7 Big Ideas (The College Board, 2014).

Table 8.1 Computational thinking progression chart

CT Vocabulary and Progression Chart					
	Definition	Grades PK to 2	Grades 3 to 5	Grades 6 to 8	Grades 9 to 12
Abstraction	Reducing complexity to define main idea	With many sizes and colours of three-sided shapes, the abstract is a triangle.	Hear a story, reflect on main items and determine a title.	After studying a period in history, identify symbols, themes, events, key people and values that are most representative of the time period (e.g. a coat of arms).	Choose a period in politics that was most like the current one by analysing the essential characteristics of the current period.

Progression Pathways, an assessment framework created by teachers Mark Dorling and Matthew Walker, has been cross-referenced to CT concepts, including abstraction (Dorling and Walker, 2014).

Abstractions vs. abstracting

The term 'abstraction' could mean the noun, a thing, such as the Tube map, or it could mean abstraction, a verb, the ability to work out what detail to include or hide in order to simplify a problem.

This might seem like a small point, but in fact it is a very important one.

Often, as we learn about new things, we are introduced to a simplified explanation of the 'thing', an abstraction. We may be blissfully unaware that there is much complexity hidden from us. For example, by following the Tube map, we are using an abstraction, not creating one. Our understanding of abstraction would, however, be developed if we were asked to evaluate the Tube map, thinking what has been included and what has been left out, and we might learn more about abstraction if we compared different maps, thinking about their different purposes and levels of detail.

Computer science abstractions

Within the world of computer science there are many, many abstractions. A computer simulation is an abstraction of a real or imaginary situation. When we learn about a computer's internal working we are asked to think of 1s and 0s. There are no little 1 and 0 numbers racing around inside our mobile devices, electrical charges make it work, but binary numbers are a clever abstraction to understand some elements of how a computer stores and manipulates data.

Keep this in mind as we turn our attention to assessing learning progression in abstraction.

Progression

The 2014 English Primary National Curriculum for Computing is only two pages long and abstraction is given the briefest of mentions as a component of the aim.

According to the *Computational Thinking – A Guide for Teachers*, abstraction is the process of making an artefact more understandable by hiding detail (Csizmadia *et al.*, 2015, p6). It is about pulling out the important details of something while suppressing or ignoring what's unimportant. As soon as we look at a problem we start to abstract, often without realising it. We create a representation of something and that representation is an abstraction: we have decided to include some aspects and hide others.

To assess children's progress in abstraction requires us to unpick the path of learning. As when assessing progression in writing, maths or science we need to understand the stepping stones of changes in knowledge, skills and understanding leading to the overall attainment target. We use our assessment to work out next steps, find barriers to learning, and design interventions, so that pupils can make progress. However, exactly what these stepping stones are for abstraction has perhaps not yet been ironed out.

Computational thinking – A guide for teachers

In *Computational Thinking – A guide for teachers* a list of distinct learner behaviours have been identified for each computational thinking concept, including abstraction. Perhaps there is an indication of progression from the order of the list (see Figure 8.5).

What each of these mean in terms of different activities and outputs across year groups has not yet been exemplified, but we can try and map the behaviours to the activities in this chapter.

- Pupils reduced complexity as they removed unnecessary detail from the sample recipes.

- They also added extra detail to get their recipe fit for purpose, but no mention is made of this as a behaviour.

- If we had modelled how to represent the recipe in a different way, such as a diagram of some kind perhaps, this might work towards 'Choosing a way to represent an artefact, to allow it to be manipulated in useful ways'.

- In Activity 3, as we hid the full complexity of an artefact, we generalised and created the basic tomato sauce 'sub-recipe'.

As we gain more experience of teaching computational thinking in primary schools, there is work to be done to provide a bank of children's work that represents these behaviours and to understand the relationship between the different computational thinking concepts.

Distinct Learner Behaviours - Abstraction

- Reducing complexity by removing unnecessary detail.
- Choosing a way to represent an artefact, to allow it to be manipulated in useful ways.
- Hiding the full complexity of an artefact (hiding functional complexity).
- Hiding complexity in data, for example by using data structures.
- Identifying relationships between abstractions.
- Filtering information when developing solutions.

(Csizmadia *et al.*, 2015)

Figure 8.5 Progression in abstraction

Progression Pathways

A second document, 'Progression Pathways with computational thinking references' (Dorling and Walker, 2014) provides an assessment framework that is peppered with the annotation 'AB' for abstraction, indicating that if a child meets one of the objectives listed in the document they have demonstrated abstraction. Each successive row or banded colour implies progression for each main column/ subheadings, but it is not clear as to whether progression in computational thinking is so simply interpreted.

For example, if we use a small sample of the Pathways document, (see Table 8.2) and try to cross-reference one or two statements marked AB to the Learner Behaviours for Abstraction identified by Csizmadia *et al.* (2015), we might not quite find a match.

Perhaps some of the statements in this document are marked as AB because they relate to children learning about an aspect of computer science using an abstraction rather than children learning about the abstraction itself.

Whether by using an abstraction we learn how to abstract is a question that is not easy to answer; it does not appear to be one of the Learner Behaviours as identified by Csizmadia *et al.* (2015). We could look to learning taxonomies such as Anderson *et al.*'s (2001) revised Bloom's Taxonomy (see Figure 8.6) and associate 'recognises' with 'remembers' and 'understands' with 'using'.

Further research is needed here in order to exemplify what is meant by each of the elements of the Progression Pathways statements and how this relates to the mapped computational thinking concepts and Learner Behaviours.

Table 8.2 Progression Pathways document

Data and Data Representation	Hardware and Processing
• Recognises that digital content can be represented in many forms. (AB) (GE)	• Understands that computers have no intelligence and that computers can do nothing unless a program is executed. (AL)
• Distinguishes between some of these forms and can explain the different ways that they communicate information. (AB)	• Recognises that all software executed on digital devices is programmed. (AL) (AB) (GE)
• Recognises different types of data: text, number. (AB) (GE)	• Recognises that a range of digital devices can be considered a computer. (AB) (GE)
• Appreciates that programs can work with different types of data. (GE)	• Recognises and can use a range of input and output devices.
• Recognises that data can be structured in tables to make it useful. (AB) (DE)	• Understands how programs specify the function of a general-purpose computer. (AB)

(Dorling and Walker, 2014)

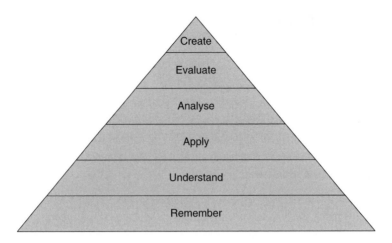

Figure 8.6 A revision of Bloom's Taxonomy

(Anderson *et al.*, 2001)

Barefoot materials

The Barefoot Primary materials afford a narrative of some of the opportunities that arise across the curriculum to indicate progression in abstraction. This narrative is based on teachers' experience rather than empirical research. A short extract is provided below.

EYFS

In early years, there are many opportunities for pupils to start to summarise. Pupils are asked to recount events and so start to think about what is important and how to create a summary. When counting they start to sense an understanding of the abstraction of number, as they count three bears, three bricks, three friends and formulate an abstraction of 'threeness'.

KS1

In Key stage 1, pupils continue to explore abstraction. They start to explore viewpoints in history as they role play famous people. They study maps in geography learning how to add places of interest and ignore detail. They use world maps and create local maps and so start to see different layers of abstraction. Written forms of abstraction become more common, for example, they abstract in literacy when they create a plan of a story; in science, when they make notes and charts as they identify what is the most important property of a material to make it suitable for a particular purpose, they are abstracting.

In computing lessons, they start to use computer games and simulations and appreciate that they are based on, but simpler than real life, i.e. an abstraction.

(Continued)

(Continued)

KS2

*In **Key stage 2**, pupils continue to simplify and summarise and in so doing become more experienced in abstraction. They reflect on what they know or have learned and create summaries, for example in pre and post topic assessments, recording the most important facts and so creating an abstraction of their understanding. Pupils may start to consider the level of detail in summaries they create. For example, they may add more detail to a story plan as they write.*

When learning about technical aspects of computers, pupils use abstractions that hide much of the detail, such as when learning about the internet, data representation or algorithms. They learn at a summary level first and then add detail as they look inside the 'black boxes' and find out more. They learn to see components of a computer or a system as 'black boxes', hiding the underlying complexity. (Barefoot, 2015)

Perhaps we can extend the Barefoot narrative of progression into the secondary phase by using the techniques of Analysing, Designing, Coding and Applying found in *Computational Thinking – A Guide for Teachers* (Csizmadia *et al.*, 2015). When analysing their requirements, whether it be for an animation, quiz, game, simulation or app, learners reduce the complexity of their project by ignoring detail they do not need. As they move to designing their solutions they *work out the structure, appearance and functionality of artifacts* (Csizmadia *et al.*, 2015) by creating computational abstractions. These abstractions include formal and informal models such as storyboards, flowcharts, pseudocode, system diagrams, data structure designs, or table layouts. As they move from design to coding, pupils implement their designs and are encouraged to use functions and procedures. These hide complexity; they are abstractions. Pupils will also be introduced to the idea of applying pre-existing solutions, design patterns, reusing and repurposing algorithms, subprograms, libraries of code into new contexts and learn to create their own generalisations.

Reflective questions

- Can you come up with a simple explanation of what abstraction is?

- Can you give three examples of how we might teach abstraction using an unplugged activity in primary schools?

- Can you think how you might change a programming project to include progression in abstraction?

Summary and Key Points

The activities in this book are based on the idea that, rather than just teaching programming, we would like children to learn to solve problems using computational thinking skills. This chapter focuses on the key problem-solving skills of abstraction, pattern and generalisation.

Abstraction is about simplifying problems by getting the right level of detail that we need to solve the task in hand: i.e. not too much detail and not too little.

We have suggested a number of unplugged activities that can be used to develop pupils' progression in the computational thinking concept of abstraction.

Across the curriculum we use abstractions to teach a whole range of ideas, from storyboards to help plan story writing to analogies and models used to learn about electricity. Within computing itself we use abstractions to learn about data, programming, hardware, communications.

We looked at how abstraction is not mentioned within the primary outcomes specifically, but is a theme in the overall curriculum aim. As one of the most important concepts within computational thinking, abstraction has perhaps been overlooked in terms of its significance for progression in learning.

Much work remains to be done in defining just what we mean by abstraction in computing at the primary level, what we might teach and how children might make progress in it.

Resources

Barefoot Project **www.barefootcas.org.uk**
A Department for Education project created to demystify computational thinking for primary teachers. Includes teach yourself concept resources and exemplar classroom activities.

Thinking Myself Kiki Pottsman (2011) **www.games.thinkingmyself.com/**
A set of online games to learn about abstraction and other computational thinking concepts.

BBC Bitesize Abstraction **www.bbc.co.uk/education/guides/zttrcdm/revision**
Overview of what abstraction is, aimed at Secondary pupils but a useful resource for teachers.

Berry, M (2014) Computational Thinking in Primary Schools Available online **http://milesberry. net/2014/03/computational-thinking-in-primary-schools** (accessed 23 December 2015).

Brennan, K and Resnick, M (2012) New frameworks for studying and assessing the development of computational thinking. Proceedings of the 2012 Annual Meeting of the American Educational Research Association, Vancouver, Canada.

Blockly Game **https://blockly-games.appspot.com/puzzle?lang=en**
An online puzzle showing a generalisation of the features of animals.

Code.org Function lesson plan **http://learn.code.org/s/1/level/46**
A lesson plan to learn about abstraction by making a suncatcher out of beads and string.

Committee for the Workshops on Computational Thinking; National Research Council. Report of a Workshop on the Pedagogical Aspects of Computational Thinking. The National Academies Press, 2011.

Computational thinking teacher resources from ISTE: **www.iste.org/explore/articledetail?articleid=152**

Deborah Seehorn, editor. K-12 Computer Science Standards – Revised 2011: The CSTA Standards Task Force. ACM, October 2011. Deborah Seehorn, Chair; CSTA – Computer Science Teachers Association.

Report of a Workshop on the Pedagogical Aspects of Computational Thinking. The National Academies Press, 2011. **www.nap.edu/catalog/13170/report-of-a-workshop-on-the-pedagogical-aspects-of-computational-thinking**

Further Reading

Armoni, M (2013) On Teaching Abstraction in Computer Science to Novices. Journal of Computers in Mathematics and Science Teaching.

Barr, V and Stephenson, C (2011) Bringing computational thinking to K-12: What is involved and what is the role of the computer science education community? *ACM Inroads*, 2(1), 48–54.

Google. (n.d.). Exploring computational thinking. Available from **www.google.com/edu/computational-thinking/**

Grover, S and Pea, R (2013b) Using Discourse Intensive Pedagogy and Android's App Inventor for Introducing Computational Concepts to Middle School Students. Proceeding of the 44th ACM technical symposium on Computer science education SIGCE. **http://dl.acm.org/citation.cfm?id=2445404**

Sentance, S and Selby C (2015) What's been done? An initial classification of research into computer science education in school from 2005–2014: Initial report (Draft).

Taub, Armoni and Ben-Ari (2012) CS Unplugged and Middle-School Students' Views, Attitudes, and Intentions Regarding CS TOCE 2011

Wing, JM (2008) Computational thinking and thinking about computing. *Philosophical Transactions of the Royal Society A: Mathematical, Physical and Engineering Sciences*, 366(1881), 3717–3725. doi: 10.1098/rsta.2008.0118 Available from **www.cs.cmu.edu/~wing/publications/Wing08a.pdf** (accessed 23 December 2015).

Wing, JM (2010) Computational Thinking: What and Why. Available from **www.cs.cmu.edu/~CompThink/resources/TheLinkWing.pdf** (accessed 23 December 2015).

Yadav, A, Mayfield, C, Zhou, N, Hambrusch, S and Korb, JT (2014) Computational thinking in elementary and secondary teacher education. *ACM Transactions on Computing Education (TOCE)*, 14(1), 5. Available from **https://w3.cs.jmu.edu/mayfiecs/pubs/2014_Yadav_CT.pdf**

References

Anderson, LW and Krathwohl, DR (eds) (2001). *A Taxonomy for Learning, Teaching, and Assessing: A Revision of Bloom's Taxonomy of Educational Objectives.* New York: Longman.

Barefoot (2015) Abstraction. Available from: **http://barefootcas.org.uk/barefoot-primary-computing-resources/concepts/abstraction/** (accessed 23 December 2015).

Beeton, I (1861) *Book of Household Management*. Available from **www.mrsbeeton.com/04-chapter4.html** (accessed 23 December 2015).

CSTA **www.csta.acm.org/Curriculum/sub/CurrFiles/CSTA_K-12_CSS.pdf**
CSTA **http://csta.acm.org/** (2014)

Csizmadia, A, Curzon, P, Dorling, M, Humphreys, S, Ng, T, Selby, C and Woollard, J (2015) *Computational Thinking – A guide for teachers*. Available from **www.computingatschool.org.uk/ computationalthinking** (accessed 23rd December 2015).

Department for Education (DfE) (2011) *Teachers' Standards*. Available from **https://www.gov.uk/ government/uploads/system/uploads/attachment_data/file/283566/Teachers_standard_ information.pdf** (accessed 23 December 2015).

Department for Education (DfE) (2013) *Computing Programmes of Study: key stages 1 and 2*. Available from **www.gov.uk/government/uploads/system/uploads/attachment_data/file/239033/PRIMARY_ national_curriculum_-_Computing.pdf** (accessed 23 December 2015).

Department for Education (DfE) (2013) *Design & Technology Programmes of Study: key stages 1 and 2*. Available from **https://www.gov.uk/government/uploads/system/uploads/attachment_data/file/239041/ PRIMARY_national_curriculum_-_Design_and_technology.pdf** (accessed 23 December 2015).

Department for Education (DfE) (2013) *English Programmes of Study: Key Stages 1 and 2*. Available from **www.gov.uk/government/uploads/system/uploads/attachment_data/file/335186/PRIMARY_ national_curriculum_-_English_220714.pdf** (accessed 23 December 2015).

Dorling, M and Walker, M (2014) *Computing Progression Pathways with Computational Thinking*. References available from **http://community.computingatschool.org.uk/resources/2324** (accessed 23 December 2015)

The College Board (2014) *AP Computer Science Principles Curriculum Framework 2016–17*. Available from **https://secure-media.collegeboard.org/digitalServices/pdf/ap/ap-computer-science-principles- curriculum-framework.pdf** (accessed 23 December 2015).

Grover, S and Pea, R (2013a) Computational thinking in K–12: A review of the state of the field. *Educational Researcher*, 42(1), 38–43. doi: 10.3102/0013189x12463051.

Chapter 9
SCIENTISTS

Equipped with his five senses, man explores the universe around him and calls the adventure Science.

Edwin Powell Hubble (May 1929)

Introduction

Science is the systematic endeavour to explain how everything in the universe works (no mean feat) and scientists are those undertaking this pursuit, developing an ever-growing body of scientific knowledge as they go. With around 7 million scientists across the globe, as a species we have amassed quite an understanding of the universe which we inhabit. Recent scientific discoveries of note include NASA's Kepler space telescope identifying a planet with similar attributes to Earth (nicknamed Earth 2) and a study at Indiana University Bloomington confirming watching cat videos is indeed good for your mood! To help organise all that we know, we have a vast range of science disciplines: supramolecular chemistry, mycology and extragalactic astronomy, to name but a few of the more obscure. However, despite the vast breadth of knowledge, there is a common single approach through which it has been built: the scientific method. While the knowing of 'scientific understanding' and the doing of the 'scientific method' are inextricably linked, it is the latter which is the focus of this chapter.

Pupils develop experience of the scientific method through the 'working scientifically' strand of the National Curriculum. The scientific method is rooted in logic, and so developing logical reasoning skills underpins pupils' ability in working scientifically. For example, scientists need to take a logical approach to experiment design in order to get useful data, and it is through logical reasoning we can analyse this data and draw conclusions as we build scientific understanding. Logic also allows us to make predictions about what we expect to happen in future investigations and explain why. In short, logical reasoning is fundamental to real-world problem solving.

Logic also underpins the workings of computers and other digital devices. Computers do not think (yet) or act differently depending on how they feel. They carry out instructions precisely as entered, in a purely logical manner. As such, when working with such technology we must adopt a logical way of thinking, just like scientists, just like 'computer scientists'.

This chapter will explore how we can develop pupils' logical reasoning and problem-solving skills in the context of science activities. Three activities are presented:

- *A drizzly bear:* learning about logical reasoning through an investigation into the best material for an umbrella.

- *Fantastic flying machines:* learning about logical reasoning through a fair test investigation into paper helicopters.

- *Spaghetti towers:* learning about the importance of perseverance in problem solving.

Lesson plan

Learning Outcomes

By the end of this chapter you will:

- understand the role of logical reasoning in the scientific method;
- understand the relevance of logical reasoning in the computing curriculum;
- be able to design unplugged activities to develop pupils' logical reasoning skills in the context of science.

Links to Teachers' Standards

The following Teachers' Standards are particularly relevant to this chapter:

TS1 Set high expectations which inspire, motivate and challenge pupils.
TS3 Demonstrate good subject and curriculum knowledge.
TS4 Plan and teach well structured lessons.

Key Stage 1

use logical reasoning to predict the behaviour of simple programs

Key Stage 2

solve problems by decomposing them into smaller parts

(DfE, 2011)

Unplugged Activity 1: A drizzly bear

Overview

In this activity pupils are posed a problem: which is the most suitable material for making an umbrella? Pupils use logical reasoning to write the algorithm for an investigation to solve this problem. Pupils also make predictions about which material they believe will be best suited, and give their reasons why. After they've conducted the investigation, pupils use logical reasoning to analyse their data and answer the problem about the most suitable material.

Computational thinking features developed

This activity develops pupils' *decomposition* skills as they break the simple investigation down into steps. As pupils write the *algorithm* for the investigation they develop their *logical reasoning* skills, since they must determine the correct order of steps. This process is similar to that discussed for programming robots in Chapter 1; however, here the process allows us to solve a real-world problem. Pupils' further exercise their logical reasoning skills as they make a prediction, giving a reason, about which material they think is best suited, and subsequently analyse the data to determine if their prediction was correct.

Cross-curricular links

Science (Working scientifically)

- asking simple questions and recognising that they can be answered in different ways

- observing closely, using simple equipment

- performing simple tests

- identifying and classifying

- using their observations and ideas to suggest answers to questions

- gathering and recording data to help in answering questions.

Science (Content)
Year 1 – Everyday materials

- describe the simple physical properties of a variety of everyday materials

- compare and group together a variety of everyday materials on the basis of their simple physical properties.

Year 2 – Use of everyday materials

- identify and compare the suitability of a variety of everyday materials, including wood, metal, plastic, glass, brick, rock, paper and cardboard for particular uses

Literacy
This activity provides the opportunity to target several strands of the English curriculum including 'Writing – composition' and 'Writing – vocabulary, grammar and punctuation'.

Age range

This activity is aimed at Key Stage 1 pupils.

Lesson plan

Learning objectives

Computational thinking

- understand what algorithms are
- use logical reasoning to write an algorithm for a simple investigation

Science

- perform a simple test
- use observations and ideas to suggest answers to questions

Key words and questions

algorithm – a precise sequence of instructions or set of rules for getting something done

decomposition – the process of breaking down a problem into smaller manageable parts

logical reasoning – helps us explain why something happens and make predictions

- How can we test which is the best material to make an umbrella from?
- What equipment will we need? Why?
- What do we need to do first/second/next? Why?
- Which material do you think would be the most suited for an umbrella? Why?
- What did you find out? How do you know?
- Which material do you now think is the most suited for an umbrella? Why?

Activities

Time	Teacher activity	Student activity	Resources
10 mins	Introduce investigation stimulus, e.g. Barnaby Bear is off on an adventure and we need to make him an umbrella. Discuss what investigation we need to conduct to find out which material is suitable.	Think-pair-share with their partner about how to complete simple investigation to find the best material. Rehearse orally with partner the steps in the investigation.	Introduction presentation, other stimulus material, e.g. bear to keep dry. Selection of materials to test and other apparatus, such as beakers and tray to catch water, etc.
10 mins	Model writing first steps in algorithm for investigation. Focus on correct logical order – think aloud through steps to model reasoning.	Pupils further rehearse steps in investigation. Pupils complete algorithm for investigation. Pupils check through each others' algorithms. Are they correctly sequenced? How do they know? Pupils make prediction.	Flipchart, paper and pens. Writing frame if required. See support section.
30 mins	Model conducting experiment. Highlight importance of logically following steps in algorithm.	Pupils conduct experiment in pairs, small groups or as class depending on organisation to suit.	Experiment equipment. Enough to suit organisation of groups.
10 mins	Lead class discussion, analysing results.	Pupils write up conclusions about which material is best suited giving reasons and use their developing scientific understanding to explain why.	

Success criteria and assessment

If pupils have met the learning outcomes, they will:

- understand that the order of steps in their algorithm is important;

- have used logical reasoning to write a correctly sequenced algorithm for their investigation;

- have followed their algorithm accurately to conduct their investigation;

- have used logical reasoning to draw a conclusion as to which is the best material for the umbrella.

Questioning can be used to elicit pupils' understanding of the importance of a correctly sequenced algorithm. Pupils' written algorithms and conclusions can be used to provide evidence against the success criteria points above. In addition, observation of pupils conducting the investigation can provide evidence as to their ability to follow the steps logically.

Scope for differentiation and extension

Support

Pupils requiring support can be given simple investigation steps, which they need to order. In making their predictions, pupils can be supported by prompting them to think about how other waterproof materials are similar to those being tested. If available, they could be further supported by a TA.

Stretch

Pupils can be challenged to think logically about what further detail should be added to their algorithm. Have they included details about the size of the material to be tested, for example? Why would this be important? Have they thought about the amount of water to use? Does this need to be the same? While 'fair testing' is not the focus here, prompts such as this can lead into a discussion about the importance of fair testing in scientific investigations for those pupils that are ready to access this.

The investigation of the suitability of materials for different purposes presents a range of cross-curricular links, for example:

- What's the best material for curtains to block out the sun?

- What's the best material for a gymnast's leotard?

- What's the best material for building a bridge over the sandpit?

Unplugged Activity 2: Fantastic flying machines

Overview

Fair test investigations are often used in solving real-world problems. Logical reasoning allows scientists to determine the relationship between two variables in a fair test investigation. For example, we might want to see how effective a variety of fertilisers (independent variable) are at enhancing crop growth (dependent variable). Here we could conduct a fair test experiment where we change the fertiliser type and measure the difference on crop production. So long as we have kept all other variables constant, we can use logical reasoning to draw a conclusion from our data about which fertiliser is the most effective.

In this activity pupils develop their logical reasoning skills in the context of a fair test investigation. The investigation uses paper helicopters, such as the one shown in Figure 9.1. Pupils formulate a scientific question they would like to answer, such as 'How does the length of the blades affect the time it takes to fall?' Pupils use logical reasoning to consider how they can solve this problem efficiently using the least amount of resources. After they have conducted the investigation, pupils draw upon

Figure 9.1 Pupil with paper helicopter

their knowledge of statistics to plot a graph of the data they record, and then use logical reasoning to interpret this data to draw a conclusion.

Computational thinking features developed

Logical reasoning plays a large part in this activity. Pupils must think logically about the sequence of steps (*algorithm*) in solving their problem. They must analyse the helicopter and reason what must be kept constant for their investigation to be a fair test – mirroring the process followed by 'real-world' scientists. In the process of working out the steps in the experiment and considering all the variables which could be altered on the helicopter, pupils are *decomposing*. Pupils may spot *patterns* in their investigation. For example, test X length blade, shorten the blade by Y, then test again. Pupils can be challenged to find the most efficient solution, in terms of time and resources, to solving their problem. For example, is it really the most efficient approach to make a new helicopter for each blade length? How could we do this better?

Pupils can be encouraged to make a *logical* prediction. They might, for example, draw on their knowledge from a previous investigation into the size of parachutes and reason that a larger blade would cause the helicopter to fall slower due to increased air resistance. If they find this prediction to be true, then *pattern spotting* between conclusions from investigations helps build scientific understanding, and further build prediction skills in the future: *I think the car with the square front will go slower in the wind tunnel because it has a bigger area for air resistance – it's like the helicopter and the parachute investigations we did!*

Cross-curricular links

Science (Working scientifically)

- Planning different types of scientific enquiries to answer questions, including recognising and controlling variables where necessary.

- Taking measurements, using a range of scientific equipment, with increasing accuracy and precision, taking repeat readings when appropriate.

- Recording data and results of increasing complexity using scientific diagrams and labels, classification keys, tables, scatter graphs, bar and line graphs.

- Reporting and presenting findings from enquiries, including conclusions, causal relationships and explanations of and degree of trust in results, in oral and written forms such as displays and other presentations.

Science
Year 5 – Forces

- Explain that unsupported objects fall towards the Earth because of the force of gravity acting between the Earth and the falling object.

- Identify the effects of air resistance.

Mathematics
This activity provides pupils with the opportunity to develop their graph plotting and interpretation skills from the statistics strand of the National Curriculum:

- Interpret and construct line graphs and use these to solve problems;

- Calculate and interpret the mean as an average.

English
Depending on how pupils are asked to present their conclusions, this activity provides scope for pupils to develop their composition skills.

Age range

This activity is intended for upper Key Stage 2 pupils.

Lesson plan

Learning objectives

Computational thinking

- use logical reasoning to plan an effective and efficient fair test investigation
- use logical reasoning to make a prediction
- use logic to deduce a causal relationship

Science

- plan, do and review a fair test investigation

Key words and questions

algorithm – a precise sequence of instructions or set of rules for getting something done

decomposition – the process of breaking down a problem into smaller manageable parts

logical reasoning – helps us explain why something happens and make predictions

pattern – when we spot and use similarities

- What can we change on the helicopter?

- What can we measure?

- What must we keep the same? Why?

- What is your scientific question?

- What is your prediction? Explain your reasoning for why you think that. Have we done anything similar before?

- How are you going to conduct your investigation? Why are you going to do it that way?

- What resources are you going to need?

- Is there a quicker way? Is there a more efficient way which uses fewer resources?

- How are you going to record/present your data?

- What is the answer to your investigation question? How do you know? Why do you think this is?

- What would you do differently next time? Why?

Activities

Time	Teacher activity	Student activity	Resources
10 mins	Introduce lesson. Show stimulus of paper helicopters. Give time for pupils to explore them.	Explore use of paper helicopters. Think-pair-share all possible variables. Think-pair-share all things which could be measured.	Paper helicopters (search online for 'paper helicopter' for template).
5 mins	Model formulating investigation question. **Note**: *this is typically exploring the effect of a variable on time to fall.* Model making a logical prediction drawing on scientific understanding.	Decide investigation question and make a prediction *with* reasoning. Record these. **Note**: *this activity could be repeated several times investigating different variables.*	
20 mins	Group pupils based on investigation question. Model writing investigation plan, focus on logical and efficient approach.	Pupils plan investigation. Challenge groups to ensure they have found the most efficient approach. Pupils' plans include details on the measurements to take and how to record their data.	
25 mins		Pupils conduct experiment and record data.	
15 mins	Lead class discussion in which groups of pupils share their data. Model drawing logical conclusion from data.	Pupils analyse their data and draw logical conclusion in response to their scientific question. Pupils use their developing scientific understanding to explain why this happened, e.g. the greater size of blade meant there was more air resistance so it fell slower.	
15 mins	Model reflecting on and evaluating the investigation. Encourage the recognition of similarities with previous investigations and wondering about what the experiment might relate to in the future.	Pupils evaluate the quality of their investigation. What would they do differently next time? Why? Are they confident in their results? Why? Can pupils spot any similarities with the result of this experiment and previous experiments? Can they think how we might use this information in the future? Have they developed their scientific understanding from this investigation? How?	

Success criteria and assessment

If pupils have met the learning outcomes, they have:

- created a scientific investigation question;

- designed a logical and efficient fair test to answer their question;

- conducted the fair test accurately and recorded their data;

- plotted and analysed their results to draw a logical conclusion to their question.

Evidence for the success criteria can be gathered from pupils' recordings of their investigation, the class discussions, observing pupils throughout the lesson and targeted questioning.

Scope for differentiation and extension

Support

Scaffolding the investigation question by specifying what will be measured can support pupils, as can providing key steps in the investigation process. Grouping pupils with more confident peers can provide support during the investigation and when analysing data. Teaching Assistant support should be directed as required.

Stretch

As pupils analyse the results, they should notice a relationship between their independent and dependent variables – they are pattern spotting. Once they have identified this pattern, challenge pupils to create a logical prediction for a measurement of their independent variable they have not yet tested, then test it and see how close they were. For example, if they have tested the effect of wingspan on time to descent for wingspans of 1cm to 5 cm, can they use logical reasoning to interpret their data to predict how long a helicopter with 0.5 cm wingspan or 7 cm might take to fall?

There is vast scope for fair test investigations linking to a variety of topics, for example:

- Investigating which shoes have most grip on an icy day
- Whether heavier people fall further on a bungee jump.
- How changing parts of a circuit affects the brightness of a bulb.

Unplugged Activity 3: Spaghetti towers

Overview

In this activity, we move into the realms of engineering, as pupils work in groups to undertake a tower building challenge. Their construction materials consist of spaghetti and marshmallows. The aim is simple: to build the tallest possible tower in the time available. A photo of a typical group's entry appears in Figure 9.2. This activity aims to develop *perseverance*: an attribute important to real-world problem solving.

Computational thinking features developed

This activity develops several computational thinking skills, particularly the importance of *perseverance* in problem solving. Given the tools pupils are given to work with, this task is quite a tricky (and sticky) one. Pupils must stick at the task, trying different methods and structures in using the resources. *Pattern spotting* is important here, since when pupils start to recognise the best way to join the spaghetti beams,

Figure 9.2 Spaghetti tower

they can repeat this method to build a stronger structure. For pupils to identify which parts of their structure is strong enough, they must be regularly reflecting and *evaluating* their work. When working as a team, pupils often naturally *decompose* the task, for example by working on different parts of the structure.

Cross-curricular links

Science
Year 5 – Properties and changes of materials

- compare everyday materials on the basis of their properties

Design and Technology
Key Stage 2.

- apply their understanding of how to strengthen, stiffen and reinforce more complex structures

Age range
Key Stage 2

Lesson plan

Learning objectives

Computational thinking

- persevere to construct a tower using the tools available
- evaluate their structure to explain what did/didn't work
- spot patterns and reuse ideas that work

Design and Technology

- apply their understanding of how to strengthen, stiffen and reinforce more complex structures

Key words and questions

perseverance – never giving up, being determined, resilient and tenacious

evaluation – is about making judgements, in an objective and systematic way where possible

pattern – when we spot and use similarities

- How are you creating your structure?

- Why are you doing it this way? Have you tried it any other way? What is/isn't working?

- Could you try it a different way?

- How have you shown perseverance?

- What are you going to try next? Why?

- Have you spotted what works well? How have you/could you use that again?

Activities

Time	Teacher activity	Student activity	Resources
10 mins		Tinker time: give pupils time to tinker with the spaghetti and marshmallow resources. How can they use them to build something? How can they join the spaghetti with the marshmallows?	Packs of spaghetti and marshmallows for each group.
5 mins	Introduce the tower building challenge. Explain that often problems, like this one, can be quite tricky! Introduce the learning objectives. Discuss the meaning of perseverance, i.e. keeping going and trying different ideas.	Give pupils plenty of time to tackle the task.	

Time	Teacher activity	Student activity	Resources
30 mins	Circulate around the groups as they are tackling the tasks. Identify traits of perseverance, e.g. trying lots of different approaches, keeping going. Stop the class for mini-plenaries to highlight examples of this.	Pupils to reflect against learning outcomes. How have they shown perseverance?	
5 mins	Determine the winning team with the highest tower!	Ask pupils to share the strategies which helped them to succeed. Groups to share what did and didn't work and what they might change if they were to tackle the challenge again.	

Success criteria and assessment

If pupils have met the learning outcomes, they will:

- have been engaged throughout the process of the task;
- have remained curious throughout the process of the task as to how best to tackle the challenge;
- have changed their approach during the task based on the evaluations they are making.

This task is about process rather than outcome. It could be that the most persistent of groups fail to make a tower of any reasonable height. As such, evidence for assessment of this task should be gathered through observation of pupils during the activity, as opposed to assessment of the outcome.

Scope for differentiation and extension

Support

- Some pupils may require additional support. These pupils could work in a group with additional adult support. The additional adult could prompt the group with ideas of what to try, so helping them to persevere. Alternatively, the group could be provided with ideas to help them build a successful tower, such as the importance of triangulating structures.

Stretch

- This task can be made more difficult by limiting the resources groups have. In making the task more difficult, this demands greater perseverance from pupils. Alternatively, once pupils have started the task and identified a way of building their tower, key resources can be removed. This sense of 'being set back' requires pupils to be resilient and persevere to find a new solution.

Variations to try:

- building a bridge to carry a load;
- building an aircraft to carry a load the longest distance.

Discussion

Key concept: logic in science

We can trace the study of logic back to early civilisations in Greece, India and China. Aristotle, who lived around 350 BC, was responsible for developing the early formal rules of logic.

Aristotle's work focused on deducing conclusions from information we already know, and so advancing our knowledge. A classic example being:

All men are mortal.

Socrates is a man.

Therefore, Socrates is mortal.

In this example, we know that 'All men are mortal' and 'Socrates is a man'; these are called premises. And from this information we can deduce some new information that: 'Socrates is mortal'. This is called deductive reasoning, as we deduce our conclusion from the information we have. Another form of logic is inductive reasoning. Here, premises provide strong evidence for a conclusion being correct, however it could still be wrong. For example, it was once thought that since all the swans that had been observed were white, then *all* swans must be white. Black swans (*Cygnus atratus*) were subsequently discovered and so this proved to be untrue.

Scientists, including our young scientists in schools, use an entangled mixture of both deductive and inductive reasoning in the process of 'doing science'. For example, we make predictions from general theories using deductive reasoning. NASA might, for example, have made this prediction during the Apollo program:

Gravity is proportional to mass and the moon has a smaller mass than the Earth so objects will fall to the surface of the moon slower than on the Earth.

Just as NASA's prediction above was rooted in their understanding of gravity, the predictions pupils make will be based on their own theories about how the world around them works. It is likely, however, that these theories will include misconceptions, and it is through the process of science enquiries that pupils get the opportunity to test these theories and refine them if necessary. For example, the pupil exploring magnets in the image below might believe:

Metal things are attracted to magnets and everything in this tray is made from metal, so I predict everything in this tray will be attracted to the magnet.

Since the tray contains aluminium objects the pupil will soon be forced to adapt their theory! As they do so, they will use logical reasoning to determine how they need to change their theory to accommodate what they have observed. They now have a new,

Figure 9.3 Pupil exploring magnets

more complete but not necessarily entirely correct, theory developed through inductive reasoning. The scientific method, and advancement of scientific understanding both in pupils and scientists, relies on this constant interplay between inductive and deductive logical reasoning.

Why logical reasoning is important

As discussed in the introduction, computers are purely logical devices. They don't behave differently depending on how they feel. If a computer is given the same set of instructions (program) and is given the same input you are very likely to get the same output. This make them predictable, and it is logical reasoning which allows us to work out what they will do. Conversely, when they are not doing as expected, it is logical reasoning which allows use to think through the algorithm or program to locate the error and fix it – a process called debugging.

In addition to science and computing, logical reasoning underpins many other subjects. In design technology for example, pupils reason about what material to use; in English pupils make predictions about what might happen in stories based on their understanding of the characters and text type; and in history they develop an understanding of the logical connections between cause and effect and how this has shaped history.

Progression in logical reasoning

The Barefoot Computing project (**www.barefootcas.org.uk**) developed a range of resources discussing each of the computational thinking and computer science concepts covered in the computing curriculum. This includes a description on the development of each computational thinking concept through the primary phase. The Barefoot Computing progression of development in logical reasoning is used below.

EYFS

As pupils' senses allow them to explore the physical world around them, they reason about what they experience. Teachers engineer a range of experiences to enhance this experience. This can be through water areas, sand areas or mini-world areas, or by providing a selection of digital devices, such as iPads, computers or floor turtles. Pupils' time is spent playing with these as they build up an understanding of how they work.

Key Stage 1

Part of the computing curriculum requires pupils to use logical reasoning to predict the behaviour of simple programs. This could include predicting how a floor turtle might move or what a sprite in a simple programming language such as ScratchJr might do when code is run. For an unplugged approach, pupils can predict the output of algorithms, for example can they work out what an algorithm might draw, or what game is described from the rules.

Key Stage 2

Pupils could be given a range of algorithms to explore, using logical reasoning to 'think through' each step in order to predict what the outcome of the algorithms might be. Importantly, pupils should be able to explain their predictions. Games and puzzles, such as Sudoku, noughts and crosses or battle ships provide plenty of opportunity for pupils to develop their reasoning. In playing these games pupils can be encouraged to explain the reasoning behind their steps or predict what their opponent might do next and, importantly, explain why. A quick online search for logic puzzles for children will reveal a vast range of puzzles designed to nurture pupils' reasoning skills.

When algorithms or programs contain bugs, pupils should be encouraged to use logical reasoning to 'think through' each step logically to detect the location of the error. As programs can often become quite complex quite quickly, pupils may decompose a program down into smaller elements first, testing each in turn to help in the debugging process. This process of decomposition also requires pupils to think logically about the most suitable place to split the program. Once they have identified the cause of the error, pupils can use logical reasoning to work out how this should be fixed and be able to explain the change they have made.

Reflective questions

- How would you describe logical reasoning?

- How is logical reasoning used in science enquiry?

- What other examples of logical reasoning have you seen across the curriculum? In maths, for example? Or in design technology?

- How can you encourage pupils to develop their logical reasoning skills?

- How is logical reasoning used in computing?

Summary and Key Points

This book provides a range of activities to help develop pupils' computational thinking skills. The focus of this chapter has been on that of logic. Logical reasoning helps us to explain why something happens and make predictions.

This chapter has illustrated how logical reasoning is at the heart of the scientific method, allowing scientists (and pupils) to both generate and test theories about the world. Science and engineering activities have been presented to help develop pupils' logical reasoning skills, as well as their perseverance.

The importance of logical reasoning in computing has been discussed and it has also been highlighted that logical reasoning is of value across a range of other curriculum subjects.

A progression in logical reasoning from EYFS to Key Stage 2 has been provided which includes ideas on what this computational thinking skill might look like through the primary phase and includes ideas for developing it further.

Resources and further reading

Barefoot Project www.barefootcas.org.uk
A Department for Education project created to demystify computational thinking for primary teachers. Includes teach yourself concept resources and exemplar classroom activities.

BBC Bitesize Key Stage 2 on Computer Science www.bbc.co.uk/guides/zxgdwmn

A set of short videos explaining critical thinking: http://io9.gizmodo.com/5888322/critical-thinking-explained-in-six-kid-friendly-animations
www.quora.com/How-many-academic-scientists-are-there-in-the-world-Said-another-way-what-is-the-total-number-of-scientists-worldwide-who-publish-their-work

Berry, M (2014) Computational Thinking in Primary Schools. Available online. http://milesberry.net/2014/03/computational-thinking-in-primary-schools

Quickstart Primary Handbook www.quickstartcomputing.org
A Department for Education and Microsoft project helping teachers deliver CPD for primary and secondary computing.

References

Department for Education (DfE) (2011) *Teachers' Standards*. Available from www.gov.uk/government/uploads/system/uploads/attachment_data/file/283566/Teachers_standard_information.pdf

Department for Education (DfE) (2013) *Computing Programmes of Study: key stages 1 and 2*. Available from www.gov.uk/government/uploads/system/uploads/attachment_data/file/239033/PRIMARY_national_curriculum_-_Computing.pdf

Department for Education (DfE) (2013) *Science: Key Stages 1 and 2*. Available from https://www.gov.uk/government/uploads/system/uploads/attachment_data/file/425618/PRIMARY_national_curriculum_-_Science.pdf

INDEX